MW00396332

WILD
BREWS

WILD BREWS

The craft of home brewing, from sour
and fruit beers to farmhouse ales

JAEGA WISE

KYLE BOOKS

An Hachette UK Company
www.hachette.co.uk

First published in Great Britain in 2022
by Kyle Books, an imprint of Octopus Publishing
Group Limited
Carmelite House
50 Victoria Embankment
London EC4Y 0DZ

www.kylebooks.com

ISBN: 978 0 85783 781 3

Distributed in the US by Hachette Book Group,
1290 Avenue of the Americas, 4th and 5th Floors,
New York, NY 10104

Distributed in Canada by Canadian Manda Group,
664 Annette St., Toronto, Ontario, Canada M6S 2C8

Publisher: Joanna Copestick
Senior Commissioning Editor: Louise McKeever
Designer: Paul Palmer-Edwards
Illustrations: Paul Palmer-Edwards
Photography on pages 2, 6–7, 35, 54–55, 58, 88, 97,
110, 186–7: Brent Darby
   (*see page 192* for all other picture credits)
Production: Lisa Pinnell

A Cataloguing in Publication record for this title is
available from the British Library.

Printed and bound in China

10 9 8 7 6 5 4 3 2 1

CONTENTS

INTRODUCTION

My first experience of cask beer was at the Loughborough Polish Club, where CAMRA held one of their many annual beer festivals. I was given a glass, some tokens and a piece of paper that listed all the available beers. Tentatively, I went through the list and eventually settled on a Harvest Pale by local brewers Castle Rock Brewery. It was light, citrusy and gently carbonated, with a fresh, bitter edge. It was also warm. Not actually heated-warm, but still miles away from the cold, fizzy lagers I was used to. I liked it. I stayed at that beer festival till late that night. It was the beginning of my love affair with beer.

You're supposed to have grandiose memories of your first beer, and in a way, I do. Growing up in the UK's Midlands, beer to me was something you drank in tinnies with your mates in the park. It was summer 2003. I was fifteen years old and eager for life experience. I wore thick glasses and a large, full backpack, and I had never been kissed. My best friend Becca was my sidekick, or rather I was hers. She was a tad shorter than me, with mousy brown hair, and she was very pretty. My first beer was that summer: a can of Foster's lager in the park behind the big Asda with friends from school. The boys in the group were the most confident. They would take it in turns to swan into the supermarket, dressed carefully to look older so they would get served. Foster's wasn't particularly my first choice – beer wasn't really my first choice, to be honest. But, as we were at the mercy of others, Becca and I accepted our tinnies readily. Foster's soon became Carling, which then became Strongbow cider, and, in turn, Carlsberg. When we were feeling fancy, it was Grolsch. I recall, quite vividly, the following summer, we rated them. My first tasting in a way, albeit not so formal. They all decided that Grolsch was the best of the lot and Carling the worst. I remember strongly disagreeing, and it descended into a good-natured teenage argument.

CHAPMAN
& SONS
EL TEL
ATIO
BAR
KEGSTAR
BRICK BREWERY
Kegstar
KEGSTAR

A few years later, I could be found, half pint of lager in hand (I was once told that buying halves made you look more feminine), dancing to Usher's 'Yeah' with my friends in the corner of the local snooker club. I didn't know it then, but those experiences were going to shape my view of beer forever. The Midlands is a place full of beer – whether the good, the bad or the ugly, it's always beer.

I was born in Woolwich, southeast London. My family moved to Nottingham when I was a baby. At the time, I had two older brothers and an older sister. My parents were in the throes of a divorce, and some of my earliest memories are of the two of them arguing. When I was three or four years old, my mum took us to live in Trinidad and Tobago in the Caribbean, to start again, I assume. My early memories are full of life in Trinidad: from full, sweet, ripe mangoes to the harsh cane licks disguised as discipline. I missed my granny a lot, and remember the packages she used to send us filled with British biscuits.

I'm not sure why we came back – I've never asked. My mum had married again and had just given birth to my little sister. I remember well the shock of our return to England. It was cold – really cold. We moved back to Nottingham and in with Granny. At school, I was a weirdo, with Trinidadian habits that were not quite the same as those of the children of Nottingham. I was also clearly academically ahead. We moved around a lot after that, all over Nottingham. In total, I went to six different primary schools. They were mostly Catholic, but one was secular, Radford Primary. There I learned to play steel drums and had a best friend, a Hindu girl called Hemangi. I remember this school vividly. It was very different from the rest. There, I was introduced to other religions and different cultures. There were many children with disabilities, and I was quickly given the task of helping them with their reading. It was a poor area. For those of you that don't know Nottingham, Radford is one of the most deprived areas in the city.

By the time I got to secondary school, I was bright and minimally damaged. My mum's second marriage was long over, and I was now one of eight children. I thrived in maths and the sciences, and was fiercely competitive in sports. I was one of the 'free school meal' kids, but I never let it bother me. In fact, the government support allowed me to do many things. I spent my EMA

(Educational Maintenance Allowance) on driving lessons and got a grant to go to university. Throughout the years, my dad used to visit. He lived in Hull, and we sometimes used to go there, but mostly he came to Nottingham. We used to go out at the weekends to watch movies, go to Burger King, bowling and the like. My dad was a very intelligent man. He had a PhD in Physics and was often the smartest person in the room. I admired him greatly, and was devastated at his premature death at the age of forty-two. I was just sixteen years old.

I remember choosing what course I should study at university. It was between English and a subject I didn't really know anything about, Chemical Engineering. I really did consider studying English: I love to read. But I think my dad's legacy shaped the way I wanted to be viewed in the end. I liked being a scientist. I liked the feeling it gave me. Chemical Engineering it was.

Studying engineering really helped me. It taught me how to be methodical and logical, and how to problem-solve and think creatively. It also taught me how to use pumps and heat exchangers. It set me up perfectly for the technical side of brewing. I didn't know it at the time, but I was building my foundations for a career in the beer industry.

I moved to London in 2010. At the time, there were fourteen breweries in the capital. The Kernel Brewery was only just beginning and Camden Town Brewery was in its infancy. Wild Card Brewery started a couple of years later in 2012. First, we were based in our living room, then in the dingy cellar of a pub in Walthamstow, east London, where we swapped casks in exchange for rent. We quickly outgrew that space and moved to the Ravenswood Industrial Estate, in the posh part of E17 known as 'Walthamstow Village'.

All the while, the UK craft beer scene was bubbling underfoot. We were neighbours to Hackney Brewery, Brodies, Redemption, Beavertown, East London Brewery and a whole host of others. It was a very exciting time, with new breweries popping up across the country on what felt like a weekly basis. And we worked hard. Probably the hardest I've ever worked. Brew shifts. Bar shifts. Delivery shifts. Then all over again. Speak to any brewer, in any brewery across the world, and they'll tell you it's anything but easy work.

As of 2020, there are 129 breweries in London. That gives you an idea of the growth: 115 new breweries have been started in the capital in as little as a decade. London was by no means in isolation: this pattern was repeated throughout the country. It was a real British brewing boom.

In that time, I've brewed cask beers, lagers, pale ales, IPAs, stouts, barrel-aged beers, sours, low-ABV (alcohol by volume) beers and high-strength beers. I've bottled, kegged and canned, and brewed Belgian styles, German styles, American styles and historical styles. I've homebrewed, cuckoo-brewed, brewed on 20-litre kits and 10,000-litre kits, and many in between. I've done multiple collaborations and judged numerous competitions all over the world. I was lucky enough to be named the UK's Brewer of the Year in 2018. There is no higher honour as a brewer – it's like the brewing Oscars, if you will.

Today, I am the Head Brewer at Wild Card Brewery, and in this book, I'm going to show you my tricks, tips and homebrew recipes. Although pale ales, stouts and everything in between are joys to brew, traditional 'ales' are not to be the focus of this book. We are going to be delving into the world of funk, into pellicles, bacteria and Brettanomyces – things that make beer sour. We are going to explore the joy that is barrel ageing and look at uncontrolled and wild fermentations. These beers are often seen as the pinnacle of brewing knowledge and prowess. They are viewed as mysterious by many, and finding books that contain all this information is difficult. I live a train journey away from Belgium, and am very lucky that I have ready access to some of the best wild brews in the world. I hope to share my love, enthusiasm and experiences with these beers.

I recently had the opportunity to recreate a historical beer, a Tudor ale, for a BBC TV show. I love a challenge, so I set about researching ale recipes from the Tudor period in earnest. Tudor ales were brewed using malt that was typically dried with wood fires, which meant the malt would take on a smoky flavour. So that's where we started. Using a hastily constructed smoker, I fired my base malt over wood chips. The ale turned out brown and smoky, and it soured quickly. We know that the technology needed to produce pale malt didn't come until much later, hence the colour of the ale. The sourness, however, was interesting. My Tudor ale didn't contain any hops, which are antibacterial in nature. Instead, it was made with a mixture of herbs and

#	Beer	Style	Brewery	ABV	Price
1	Chateau Neubourg Pilsener		Gulpener	5.5%	€2,90 20cl
2	GERARDUS BLOND		Gulpener	6.5%	€4.65 25cl
3	GERARDUS DUBBEL		GULPENER	7%	€4.90 25cl
4	GERARDUS TRIPEL		GULPENER	8.5%	€4.90 25cl
5	KORENWOLF	Witbier	Gulpener	5%	€4.65 30cl
6	ONGEFILTERDE DORT	ongefilterde dortmunder	Gulpener	7.5%	€5.50 25cl
7	Lentebock	LENTEBOCK	GULPENER	6.5%	€5.40 25cl
8	SKUUMKOPPE	Dunkel Weizen	Texelse	6%	€4.65 30cl
9	MISS SAISON	SAISON	JOPEN	7%	€5.15 cl
10	Totally Yuzu	CASCADIAN DARK ALE	Jopen	7%	€5,15 25cl
11	MOOIE NEL	IPA	JOPEN	6.5%	€4.90 25cl
12	EXTRA STOUT	STOUT (ON NITRO)	Jopen	5.5%	€4.65 25cl
13	DRUNK PANETTONE	BELGIAN QUAD.	KEES! BIRRANOVA	10%	€5,- 15cl
14	Saens Wit	WITBIER	Breuben	4.3%	€4.90 25cl
15	DIPA	DIPA	de Prael	9%	€5,50 25cl
16	Koning Honing	honey ale	SNAB	7.5%	€5.15 cl
17	ONE KNIGHT IN BRETT	BRETT STRONGALE	LECKERE	11%	€4.70 15cl
18	THAI THAI	TRIPEL	OEDIPUS	8.0%	€4.90 25cl
19	DUTCH EAGLE PALE ALE		MORE...		
20	IPA		BRUUT		
21	Dunckel Bier	keller	Langweiner & Sisters		
22	Mikkie = Cattivella	Crème Brûlée Imperial Stout	Ma... + Di...		
23	Keizer Tamarin	NORTH WEST IPA	RANS... de BeBaa...		
24	Kicking Kohatu Kangaroo	NZ Dad & Lu...			
	gespoeld 13-5				
26	GAJES	TRIPEL	BRUUT	8	
27	RYPER LIEFDE	Red ale	Leeghwater		
28	CASCADIAN DARK ALE	CASCADIAN DARK ALE	WENTERSCH	5.	
29	BALLAST	Weizen	Kompaan		
30	ASIAN WHITE	WIT BIER	BREUGEM		
31	PRELOAD	IPA	Oersoep		
32	Cascade Green Sweater	DIPA	Uie...		
33	Dirty Katarr...	JAMESON BA IMP STOUT	TWO CHEFS BREWIN...		
34	Heavy Apple	cider	Uwe		
35	BARREL PROJECT	JACK DANIELS BA PORTER			
36	Kraints	TRIPE	OESIAT & ...TER	8	

spices known as a 'gruit'. In addition, it was common to store beer in wooden barrels, which almost certainly would have been riddled with microbes. In all likelihood, Tudor ale would have soured quickly. When I tasted the beer, it tasted so familiar, yet so foreign to my twenty-first-century palate. Our modern tastes are comparatively banal, I'm sure. Now, we are so used to clean brewing, with our stainless-steel vessels and our sterilising sprays. Long ago, long before brewing hygiene was fully understood, most ales would have had some semblance of funk. It's this funk we are looking to understand – and to exploit.

One of my first wild brews was De Ranke's Kriek. An intense, deep red, cherry-blended lambic. It was superb. The beer was very fruity, but not overly sweet. In fact, it was the opposite, quite dry, with only a hint of cherry sweetness. It was sharp, sour and refreshing, with both an earthy underbelly and a vibrant cherry zing. It came wrapped in off-white thin paper, with the words 'KRIEK DE RANKE' printed on the front in large, bold red letters. Not an easy beer to walk past. I was hooked.

I would have to say one of my favourite wild beers was actually a recent one. I try to make it a point to sample something new when I'm out and about, and this time I'm especially glad I did. I'd travelled to Amsterdam, where I was invited to talk at a conference. After a long day, I popped into Proeflokaal Arendsnest, an excellent bar in the centre of the city. I would highly recommend this bar; they had fifty-two beers on tap, and two of those were cask ales. One of the cask beers jumped out to me immediately: Lambiek, by Dutch brewers Vandenbroek. The beer blew me away. It was superbly balanced: tart, but in a gentle way, and just the right combination of fruity and funky, with a strong oak backbone. The lower carbonation and higher serving temperature from the cask seemed to suit the beer beautifully, bringing out some interesting flavours I didn't even realize I'd missed in other chilled bottled lambics. I was truly in heaven that day.

When brewing wild beers, do not be afraid to ask questions. I have learned so much from others, and you can, too. Most brewers are friendly folks, and will be more than happy to offer you tips. I recently met the Mikkeller Baghaven team and asked them dozens of questions while suppin' on their Amphora fermented Danish wild ale. In essence, it's good to compare notes.

1

THE INGREDIENTS

BARLEY, WATER, HOPS & YEAST

The four ingredients needed to make beer are barley, water, hops and yeast. For the purposes of this book, I am going to briefly cover each ingredient, but I would advise anyone who is interested in brewing to read up further on all of them. To put it bluntly, you could write an entire book on each of these simple yet complex ingredients.

There are some basic rules of thumb you should follow when brewing, and it's perfectly possible to make spectacular beer without zooming in on the science.

Fermentation is by no means a new process. For as long as there have been humans, we've been finding a way to make things alcoholic – whether intentionally or not. The word 'ferment' comes from the Latin *'fervere'*, literally meaning 'to boil'. It's easy to see why one would make that connection. The process of boiling does mimic some of the physicality of an active beer fermentation, albeit without the scalding heat that usually comes with a boil. It wasn't until Louis Pasteur's work in 1876 that the role yeast played in alcohol fermentation was fully understood.

When I first started brewing, I was obsessed with wanting to control every tiny thing in the brewing process. And, to a certain extent, you probably can. Over time though, I learned that making great beer may be a science, but it is also an art. Beers today are 'cleaner' than they have ever been, but a beer can be technically flawless without necessarily being a great beer. The average adult has 2,000–4,000 taste buds on their tongue. No machine can truly replicate this. People all around the world are employed as tasters, because they can do what machines cannot. Your tongue is one of your most powerful weapons. The other is your nose. Both can be trained and moulded to learn to recognise positive and negative flavours and smells, which will help to improve your brews. I've included a chapter on negative beer flavours to guide you on this journey.

I've found this book difficult to write. I'm very aware of my background. In my very core, I am a scientist. Trying to balance that with the flowery language necessary for an entertaining recipe book has been a challenge. So, in all candour, I made a decision to be true to myself: to write the book I would have wanted to read when I was starting out on my journey into wild beers.

Yes, that does mean there is some science. I've tried to keep it to areas where it's totally relevant. Understand, though, that for me, science is not a dirty word, but a friendly one. It's an area in which I feel safe and comfortable. I'm also well aware that this may not be the case for many of you, and I would absolutely hate people to put this book down out of fear that it is too technical. So I hope that I've come to a healthy balance: that was certainly my aim. Feel free to delve straight into the recipes, or to read up more about the technical side in the subsequent chapters. That's one of the fantastic things about beer: it welcomes all.

BARLEY

Barley is a type of cereal grain. It has been grown by humans around the world for thousands and thousands of years. The primary use of barley in the brewing process is as a source of sugar. It is the brewer's job to extract the sugar from this cereal grain.

MALTING

In order for barley to be useful to the brewer, it has to go through the malting process. If you were to pick barley from the fields, then add hot water to it, very little would happen. The amount of sugar you would get out of the barley would be minimal. This is because barley in its raw form is very hard – hurt-your-teeth hard. The malting process softens the barley and makes it a sugar source accessible to the brewer.

It was down to the brewer to malt barley as well. These days, there is a whole other industry of people known as maltsters, whose job it is to do just that. They feed malted barley into the brewing industry and the whisky industry, as well as to the of all your favourite malty drinks and snacks (think Ovaltine and malted milk biscuits – nom nom).

Having a working knowledge of the malting process is useful. Prior to arriving on your doorstep, the malted barley has gone through farmers, chemical engineers, chemists and biologists, all ensuring that it has been malted in just the right way to give you the sugar you need. Barley that has been poorly malted should now be the exception rather than the rule, and simply working with a reputable maltster can help you to avoid a lot of problems.
The malting process loosely looks like this:

1. Raw barley is usually stored in dry form, so the first step is to steep the raw barley in water. The water is then drained and the barley is allowed to rest in the air. The barley is then soaked in water again. This happens several times until the desired moisture content of the barley is reached.

2. Barley begins to germinate, or to grow a little bit. A number of different enzymes are developed and the starch reserves, which the plant would ordinarily need for growth, become accessible. This is known as 'modification'.

3. Germination is purposefully stopped by applying heat and kilning the barley.

4. The barley is then dried, so its moisture content is greatly reduced.

5. The tiny rootlets growing out of the barley kernel are removed (they come off quite easily with a little agitation).

6. The barley is then sent to the brewer, either whole or pre-crushed.

THE MALTING PROCESS

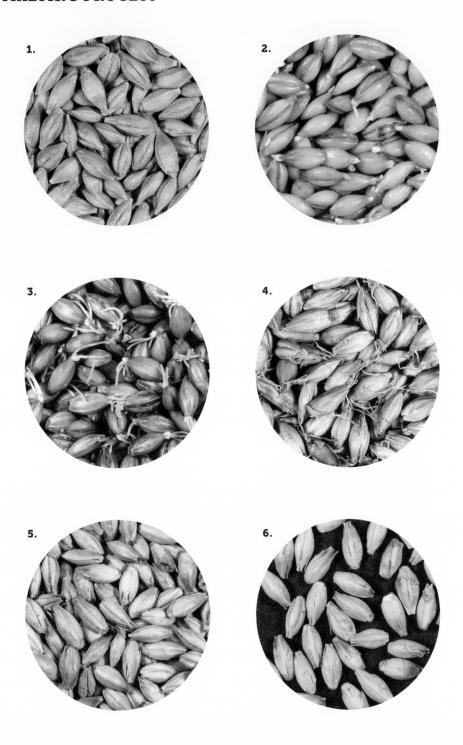

THE CRUSH

Either the maltster or the brewer will crush the grain in preparation for brewing. The aim is to break the barley kernel to give better access to the goodies contained within. It's unlikely that you'll have a grain mill at home, so it's important you buy crushed malted barley when you make your purchase.

The level to which the grain is crushed is also of importance. Is the crush fine, or is it coarse? This becomes important in both the mash and sparge stages of the brew, which I will explain below. During the mash, you mix crushed malted barley with hot water in a vessel called a mash tun. This process is commonly known as 'mashing in'. Your primary aim is the conversion of the starches and carbohydrates in your malted barley into simple sugars using the enzymes already present in the barley.

After leaving the barley and water for some time to get acquainted, you must then begin the process of separating the barley from your now sugar-laden water, which is known as the 'wort'.

More water is sprinkled over the barley to rinse off and capture any remaining sugars you've produced during the mash stage. This is known as 'sparging'. Your wort has to be able to pass through the barley, so it's important that your grain bed has good filterability. The crush of your malted barley will affect this filterability. It will also affect the amount of sugar you get per kilogram of malted barley – in other words, your mash efficiency.

A finer crush means the enzymes in your malted barley will have an easier time and more sugars will be produced, but this comes at the expense of filterability. You'll probably end up with a porridge-like mess, and it then becomes difficult to separate the grain from wort. Too coarse a crush, meanwhile, allows for greater fluid flow in between your grain, meaning you'll be able to separate the grain from the wort easily, but this is at the expense of efficiency. A compromise between the two is what you're looking for: good efficiency and good filterability.

It is common for larger microbreweries to have a mill, which means they will buy whole malted barley and dictate the crush themselves. While advantageous in terms of both cost and brewing efficiency, dictating the crush of your barley is just not an option for most homebrewers. I would probably go as far as saying crushing your barley at home is an unnecessary barrier to a new homebrewer. Although, having said that, I have met several keen homebrewers who do crush their own grain. If you've got the desire and the equipment, why not?

Do keep an eye on the quality of your crush when you receive your barley. If you're doing everything else right, but are still ending up with a grain bed that won't filter your wort, better known as the dreaded 'stuck mash', a poorly crushed barley could be the potential cause.

Opposite: A grain mill crushes the malted barley kernels directly into the mash as it is mixed with hot water.

TYPES OF MALT

There are many different types of malt used in brewing, from the lightest of pale malts to the dark, rich and intense black malt.

The foundation of any beer recipe is its base malt. The base malt makes up the majority of your brewing grain and will be responsible for a large proportion of enzymatic activity and sugar produced in your mash. Different variations in kilning in the final stages of the malting process determines the wide variety of malt colours and flavours available. The amount you kiln a malt also determines its enzyme content and therefore the amount of sugar you will get from it.

As a general rule, the lighter the malt in colour, the more sugar you will be able to extract from it. With darker malts, more enzymes are destroyed by the heating process, so these malts are used for their other attributes, mainly flavour and colour.

LAGER MALT
A malt with very low colour and high enzymatic activity, which means good sugar extraction.

PALE MALT
A low-colour malt that tends to give a light-straw to golden colour. Commonly used as a base malt, it has high enzymatic activity.

VIENNA MALT
Golden to amber in colour, this malt gives beer good body and mouthfeel. It has enough enzymatic activity to be used as a base malt, or it can be blended with other malts.

AMBER MALT

A lightly toasted malt that provides biscuity flavours, with a delicate toasted note and a crisp dryness. Dark golden to light brown in colour, this malt should be used in combination with other malts.

MUNICH MALT

This malt can add a dark golden to brown colour to your brew. It's known as being full-flavoured and rich, and brings heavy bready and malty flavours to your beer. This malt also has a high level of enzymatic activity, so is great for starch conversion into sugars.

CRYSTAL MALT

This caramelised malt adds sweet, nutty, chewy, toffee and caramel flavours to your beer. It comes in a variety of colours, from the golden caramalts to the deep red of the dark crystal malts. With the right combinations, it's fantastic for adding a true red colour to your brew.

BROWN MALT

This malt adds a smooth mouthfeel and brings nutty, chocolate and coffee flavours to dark beers. As you would expect, it adds a brown colour. When used lightly, it adds a dark amber hue.

CHOCOLATE MALT

This adds a dark chocolate flavour to your beers with low bitterness levels, and gives a rich deep-brown colour. It can make up up to 10 per cent of your malts.

BLACK MALT

The darkest of the coloured malts, this adds bitterness and intense notes of smoky coffee and cacao. It can be used lightly for its intense dark colour without the roasty flavours.

SUPPLEMENTARY INGREDIENTS (ADJUNCTS)

Although malted barley is the primary grain used in the production of beer, unmalted barley and other cereal grains, such as oats, rice, corn, rye, wheat, sorghum and millet (among others) can also be used to make beer. When they are used as a supplement ingredient to the main mash, these are known as 'adjuncts'.

UNMALTED BARLEY

ROASTED BARLEY

This unmalted barley is exactly what it sounds like: barley that has been roasted. It gives flavours of coffee and chocolate, with prominent burnt notes and a very present bitterness. It works well in combination with chocolate malt and can add an interesting complexity to your beer.

I always use a healthy amount of roasted barley when brewing a stout. Be cautious when using it in quantities above 10 per cent of your grain bill as it can very easily overwhelm and dominate a recipe.

FLAKED BARLEY

An unmalted, cooked barley that is then dried and flattened, this is great for a nice, thick, creamy head, and can add excellent body and mouthfeel to your beer. Flaked barley adds an interesting grainy flavour, but it needs to be mixed with malted grains, as it doesn't contain significant enzymes for starch conversion into sugar.

TWO-ROW OR SIX-ROW BARLEY

You may have heard of 'two-row' and 'six-row' barley. I want to touch on this briefly so you're fully prepared when making your malt purchase. Six-row barley is typically grown in the US. It contains high levels of enzymes, which means that you can mix it with flaked rice and flaked corn in the mash and still get a good efficiency. Two-row malt is what is typically grown in the UK and Europe. It has a higher carbohydrate content than six-row, and a lower enzyme content. There is also a flavour difference between the two that must be noted. US six-row tends to add a grainier flavour, whereas the European two-row adds a maltier characteristic.

Which one is better? Many times I have sat in malt conferences and heard someone proclaim that 'the UK grows the best barley in the world'. But don't just take a European's word for it. Just like the skewed version of British history I learned as part of my Catholic upbringing (Guy Fawkes was a freedom fighter, apparently), as a UK brewer, I am obviously biased. If you are interested in experimenting with different grains to supplement your main mash, like rice or corn, then by all means give six-row malt a go.

WHEAT

WHEAT MALT

Widely used in the production of wheat beers, this can be used as a base malt, forming up to 70 per cent of the main grist (the grist is the total crushed cereals used to make up your mash). Unlike barley, wheat does not contain a husk, so it suffers from poor filterability. I usually like to use wheat malt for between 40 and 45 per cent of the main grist when making a wheat-based beer to avoid issues when sparging. Wheat malt adds a haze to your beer, along with gentle bready and citrussy flavour notes. If used in small quantities, wheat malt can add body and a long-lasting head.

TORREFIED WHEAT

To 'torrefy' something means to heat it. Torrefied wheat has been heated until it 'pops', popcorn-like. This process exposes its internal starch, ready for starch conversion into sugars. Please note that torrefied wheat does require the presence of malt enzymes for starch conversion to occur. Torrefied wheat can form up to 10 per cent of your grist, but I like to use about 3 per cent for a nice, thick, creamy head. It adds a slight grainy flavour to your beer.

FLAKED WHEAT

An unmalted wheat. Added to the grist in quantities typically between 5–10 per cent, it is known for adding a crisp flavour to your beer. Good for foam stability and adds a thickness and a haze to your brew.

OATS

MALTED OATS

Malted oats are exactly that: oats that have gone through the malting process. Malted oats are very versatile and can be used in a wide variety of beers. They add a velvety mouthfeel and a silky smooth body. They can typically form up to 20 per cent of your grist. Expect lower sugar extraction in malted oats compared to malted barley.

FLAKED OATS

Flaked oats are unmalted oats that have been heat- and pressure-treated. This gelatinises the starch, making it readily available for us brewers. Commonly found as regular porridge oats in supermarkets, oats can add what can only be described as a gummy propensity to your mash. If oats make up more than about 10 per cent of your grist, you need to take steps to counteract this, otherwise you may have issues with a stuck sparge later on. Holding your mash at a temperature of 40–50°C (104–122°F) for 30 minutes, known as a 'beta-glucan rest', can help. You can also try adding rice hulls to increase your mash bed's filterability.

RYE

Rye is often used for the rich mouthfeel and full palate it gives to beer. It also imparts a distinctive spicy flavour. Rye that has been malted is common, although be aware that rye is husk-less, which means it makes poor filter material. If rye makes up more than about 20 per cent of your grist, you may want to add a mash filtration aid, such as rice hulls. Works wonderfully in malt forward beers, especially when used in conjunction with crystal rye malt.

WATER

Water is the lifeblood of beer. It makes up around 94 per cent of the content of a 5 per cent alcohol pint, yet in my experience, it is often the most overlooked brewing ingredient.

Water, in almost all naturally occurring circumstances, will contain various substances, including dissolved gases, dissolved ions, microorganisms, pollutants and physical solids to name but a few. Prior to coming out of your tap, your water will have gone through several stages of water purification. Things like physical solids, harmful bacteria and heavy metals, such as lead, should all have been removed at your local water treatment plant. Here in the UK, what comes out of our taps is safe to drink. However, drinking water still contains plenty of things, from dissolved impurities to added disinfectants. The exact composition of your water will vary from place to place.

Different beer styles have developed in different parts of the world often because of the chemical composition of the local water. It's one of the reasons why London is known for its porter and the Czech Republic is known for its Pilsner. As brewers, we try to mimic the water composition that we know will produce a particular style of beer well.

If you are at the beginning of your beer-making journey, I would suggest that brewing with pre-boiled tap water is a good place to start. Your brewing water should be clear, odourless and safe to drink. If you'd like to leave water treatment at that, then to you I say, Happy Brewing! If, however, you want to get more into the nitty gritty of water treatment, read on...

GET YOUR WATER TESTED

Water composition directly affects the flavour of beer. You could make exactly the same beer, side by side, but use different sources of water for each, and those two beers will probably taste different. Depending on the type of water in your immediate area, and the kind of beer you want to make, you will probably have to treat your water.

Knowing the chemical make-up of your water is a great place to start. Most breweries will have had their water tested at some point, and will probably be happy to share the results, so ask your local brewery for that information. If that isn't an option, talk to your water provider and they should be able to send you a report showing what's in your water. It is also relatively cheap to send a sample of your water to a laboratory for testing.

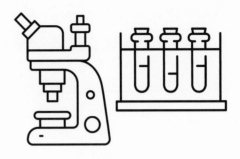

Below: It is invaluable to obtain
a laboratory analysis of your
water in order to get a detailed
breakdown of its chemical
composition.

INTERPRETING YOUR TEST RESULTS AND MAKING WATER ADJUSTMENTS

Reading a water report can be a dazzling affair. However, if you're starting with drinkable tap water, there's really no need to be dazzled, as there are only six parameters we are interested in. They are:

CHLORIDE
CL^{-1}

SULPHATE
SO_4^{-2}

ALKALINITY
$CACO^3$

HARDNESS
$CACO^3$

CALCIUM
CA^{2+}

MAGNESIUM
M^{+2}

I always find it useful to bear in mind how certain dissolved compounds present in your water will directly affect the flavour of your beer. You can use this as a rough guide:

- **Chloride** – affects the fullness, mouthfeel and body of your beer.

- **Sulphate** – affects the dryness and crispness of your beer, and accentuates hops and bitterness.

- **Alkalinity** – affects the pH: high levels can lead to flabby, dull-finished beer.

- **Hardness** – can cause scale on heating surfaces, which can lead to burnt notes on beer if left unchecked.

- **Calcium** – affects your beer's stability, clarity and flavour.

- **Magnesium** – affects the performance of your yeast, as it's an important yeast nutrient.

ADJUSTING CHLORIDE & SULPHATE

One of the easiest ways to demonstrate the effect that water treatment has on the body, balance and flavour of your beer is to change the amount of chloride and sulphate present in your brewing water.

High chloride levels add a fullness and sweetness to your beer, while high sulphate levels will add the perception of puckering dryness and a bitter accent. So, the two have opposite effects on the flavour of your beer. More important than the total sulphate and chloride content of your brewing water is the ratio between the two. A 3:1 sulphate-to-chloride ratio will generally give you a drier beer, perfectly suited to British bitters, whereas a 1:2 sulphate-to-chloride ratio will give you a much softer beer, much more appropriate for milds and the more modern, low-bitterness, heavily hopped IPAs.

I do have fun playing around with the sulphate-to-chloride ratios in my brewing water. In my opinion, adjusting this ratio can create some of the most noticeable changes in your beers. I have had particular success with a sulphate-to-chloride ratio of 1:1; I find it offers a nice compromise between the benefits of chloride and sulphate ions in your beer. In essence, feel free to play around here – there are big flavour gains to be had.

Acceptable chloride levels in your brewing water are between 0–250mg/l. Sulphate levels should be in the region of 50–350mg/l, with less bitter beers on the lower end of that scale, and the higher end reserved for beers with more prominent bitterness. You can use calcium chloride flakes to increase chloride and calcium – this will also slightly lower the pH of your mash. Calcium sulphate (gypsum) will increase your calcium and sulphate levels and add a dry crispness to your beer. Magnesium sulphate (Epsom salts) will increase the magnesium and sulphate levels of your beer, and will also help with your beer's crispness.

Sodium chloride (yes, table salt) can be a useful addition to adjust your chloride levels and increases palate fullness. Be careful to keep any sodium chloride additions to below 280mg/l to avoid your beer taking on a more 'salty' flavour.

Your local homebrewing shop will have these salts. Ask for a specification sheet, which will tell you how much you should add for an increase in the desired ion. Add your salts directly to your grain when mashing in, not to your water.

> 1mg/l=1ppm (parts per million).

ADJUSTING ALKALINITY

Alkalinity is a property of water and describes the water's ability to resist changes in pH. Low levels of alkalinity are preferred for most beer styles. Generally, you want your water to contain less than 50mg/l alkalinity ($CaCO_3$). High levels of alkalinity in your brewing water can cause a high pH throughout your brew and can lead to flavour issues, especially when making pale beers. A finished beer whose pH is too high tastes 'flabby' and unfocused – dull. And that's never a flavour we are going for.

One of the easiest ways to reduce your alkalinity is to add an acid to your brewing water. The most common options are sulphuric acid or lactic acid. Your local homebrewing shop should sell these acids, which should come with instructions for dosing rates. Lactic acid has many uses in beer making and is generally referred to as simply lactic acid. In beer circles, however, I've found that sulphuric acid is often disguised under a commercial name, so watch out for that.

It's important to remember that when acidifying your water, there is not a specific pH you need your brewing water to reach. The relationship between the pH of your brewing water and the pH of the mash is by no means a direct one. The chemistry is complex. The most important factor is the overall pH of your mash. This is one of those basic rules of thumb: if you manage to get your mash pH to between 5.2 and 5.5, you've done good.

Another technique for reducing alkalinity is to add a kilned or roasted malt to your mash. A good example of an area with high alkalinity in the water is London, where I happen to do the majority of my brewing. In order to make a porter, you require barley that has been roasted. The roasting process acidifies the malt slightly, and that acidic malt combined with high-alkaline London water creates excellent conditions to make a porter. In essence, as a homebrewer in London, you can make a cracking porter or a luscious stout without adjusting your water in any way before brewing. If you were to try to make a lager or a pale ale under the same conditions, though, it probably won't be great.

If you want to make a light beer, you can also use acidulated malt. Acidulated malt is made using lactic acid-producing bacteria. In general, 1 per cent acidulated malt in your grist will lower the pH of your mash by 0.1. In areas where there is high alkalinity, it's not uncommon for acidulated malt to form up to 10 per cent of your grain bill.

If you are brewing in an area with low alkalinity and you want to make dark beers with lots of roasted malts, you may need to increase your brewing water's alkalinity in order to get the pH of your mash into the 5.2–5.5 golden zone. You can add calcium carbonate or sodium bicarbonate (bicarbonate of soda) directly to your mash in order to raise its pH.

Buy yourself a pH meter. Hitting certain pH targets throughout your brew will let you know that you are on the right track, and this will ultimately lead to better beer. If you don't want to spend the money (and let's face it, you may not want to stretch to the expense of a pH meter if you're a casual homebrewer), then buy pH strips. They won't be as accurate, but they are cheap. You can buy narrow-band pH strips, i.e. 4.6–6.2 pH, which will keep you on track throughout your brew.

ADJUSTING HARDNESS, CALCIUM & MAGNESIUM

'Hard water' is defined as water with a high level of magnesium and calcium compounds. The most obvious sign that you are living in a hard-water area is scale in your kettle and difficulty in creating soap suds. Water with a medium level of hardness (150mg/l $CaCO_3$) actually makes quite good brewing water, as a good calcium content (50mg/l–150mg/l) aids protein precipitation in the boil and the beer's overall stability. Calcium and magnesium also play important roles as yeast nutrients. You want your magnesium levels to be in the range of 10–30mg/l. Magnesium levels above 50mg/l tend to impart a harsh, bitter, sour taste to your beer, while levels above 150mg/l can have a laxative effect.

Hardness (total hardness) can be broken down into two types: permanent hardness and temporary hardness.

Total hardness = temporary hardness + permanent hardness

TEMPORARY HARDNESS
Calcium carbonate – $CaCO^3$
Calcium bicarbonate – $Ca(HCO_3)_2$
Magnesium bicarbonate – $Mg(HCO_3)_2$

PERMANENT HARDNESS
Calcium chloride – $CaCl_2$
Calcium sulphate – $CaSO_4$
Magnesium chloride – $MgCl_2$
Magnesium sulphate – $MgSO_4$

An easy way to distinguish between temporary and permanent hardness is that temporary hardness can be removed from water just by boiling, and permanent hardness cannot. Boiling the water causes mainly calcium carbonate (or, to use its more popular name, chalk) to precipitate out of the water. When the water has cooled, it can be poured into another container to separate it from the calcium carbonate precipitate. The separated water will be left considerably softer. This method also helps to reduce your brewing water's alkalinity.

Permanent hardness is exactly that: permanent. Boiling will not remove permanent hardness. There are other methods brewers can use on a commercial scale, such as ion exchange and reverse osmosis, but these are not viable options for most homebrewers. This begs the question: why would you want to remove permanent hardness when moderate hardness is actually good for your beer? Well, some breweries find it advantageous to build their water profiles from scratch. You can use reverse osmosis, for example, to remove almost all dissolved compounds from your brewing water, then add the salts of your choosing.

By contrast, soft water can be defined as water with low levels of magnesium and calcium compounds. Rainwater is naturally soft. When this soft rainwater passes through limestone and chalk, it collects magnesium and calcium compounds, becoming hard water. In the UK, the south and east are typically the limestone and chalk areas, and tend to have hard water, while the north and west are dominated by granite, and tend to have soft water.

So, the three main water-treatment methods in your arsenal as a homebrewer are to boil your water, to acidify your water, or to add salts to your mash – or a combination of the above. In general, I would say water chemistry is an area that requires tweaking over time. Try changing one thing and see if it improves your beer. Use the levels suggested here as a starting point, but it's important that you make adjustments as you go. Small adjustments can make a big difference.

MAP OF UK'S WATER HARDNESS

● **SOFT WATER**
Less than 100mg/l
as calcium carbonate ($CaCO_3$)

● **HARD WATER**
100–200mg/l
as calcium carbonate ($CaCO_3$)

● **VERY HARD WATER**
More than 200mg/l
as calcium carbonate ($CaCO_3$)

HOPS

Hops are the female flower from the plant *Humulus lupulus*. It is a herbaceous perennial and can climb voraciously. Hops add both flavour and bitterness to beer, but they also play a vital antimicrobial role, helping to preserve beer and contribute greatly to its overall stability.

Hops contain alpha acids, which, when boiled, impart a stable bitterness into beer. We can measure the amount of bitterness a hop addition will give to a beer by tracking the alpha acid content of the hop itself, as well as the length of time the hop is boiled for. This can be expressed as an International Bitterness Unit, or IBU, and is the globally recognised way of measuring a beer's bitterness level.

Hops also contain hop oils, which are responsible for the hop aroma and flavour imparted into beer. Hop oils are naturally very volatile, which means they dissipate quickly with heat. The longer you boil a hop, the more hop aroma is lost. Brewers add hops throughout the boil stage of the brewing process in order to impart both bitterness and aroma into their beers. If you come across a beer that has a very strong hop aroma, chances are that hop has been dry hopped (see right).

Hops are typically added three to four times throughout the brew. (You will learn more about the different stages of brewing later in the book.)

BITTERING HOP – added at boil

Adds the majority of bitterness to your brew. The aroma from the hops is lost when added at this stage due to its volatility.

MIDDLE HOP – added at about 40 minutes into a 60-minute boil

Adds some bitterness and some hop aroma and flavour to your beer.

AROMA HOP – added at end of boil or whirlpool

Adds hop aroma and flavour to your beer.

DRY HOP – added to the fermenter or directly to a cask

Adds intense aroma and flavour to your beer.

Traditionally, almost all beers would have had a bittering, mid and aroma hop added. But with new brewing techniques, differences in the way we hop have also developed. I would say that almost all the hop additions in the list above are optional.

The sheer quantity of hops required to brew a New England IPA (or NEIPA for short) means that you have to use your hops efficiently. If that means removing your middle hop in favour of a dry hop instead, then so be it. The move towards beers with almost no bittering has also fuelled this trend. It is imperative to note, however, the important role that hops play in the preservation and stability of a beer. With this in mind, I do almost always add hops to the boil, no matter what I'm making, in order to aid this.

HOPS FROM AROUND THE WORLD

Hops from all around the world are known for their different characteristics, or their terroir, if you will. Differences in soil, climate and, most importantly, sunshine means that hops from different parts of the world will be wildly different. In my head, I like to characterise the positive relationship between sunshine and hop intensity. The hotter the climate, the more pungent the flavours tend to be.

By no means do all hops within a geographical area exhibit the same characteristics, but with so much hop choice on the market, it can be helpful to categorise hops according to their region to give you a great starting point. Here are some of my favourites.

BRITISH HOPS

British hops tend to bring a soft but present bitterness and are generally known for their simplicity. They make a fantastic mild or best bitter, and go wonderfully in a porter, stout or low-ABV Midlands cask pale ale. Think earthy flavours, blackcurrant and spice.

HOP	FLAVOURS	ALPHA ACID	HOP INTENSITY
Fuggles	Grassy, mint, earthy	5–7 per cent	Low
Bramling Cross	Lemon, blackcurrant, spice	5–8 per cent	Medium
Pioneer	Lemon, cedar, herbal	9–12 per cent	Medium
Target	Pine, orange, cedar	9–12 per cent	Medium
East Kent Goldings	Spice, honey, earthy	5–8 per cent	Low
Challenger	Spice, cedar, green tea	5–9 per cent	Medium

From *Well Hopped! Hop Variety Brochure*, www.charlesfaram.co.uk

AMERICAN HOPS

American hops are known for their intensity. They are loud, sometimes they are trashy, but mostly they are beautiful. American hops tend to be heavily in demand with the modern craft brewer. If you are after those big citrus notes, the intense pine, and those flavours that could only be described as 'dank', then American hops are the ones for you. They include the world's most famous hop, Citra. Now Citra, in my opinion, is the queen of the aroma hop, and generally an all-round badass.

HOP	FLAVOURS	ALPHA ACID	HOP INTENSITY
Citra	Mango, grapefruit, lime	11–14 per cent	High
Cascade	Lychees, floral, grapefruit	5–9 per cent	Medium
Williamette	Blackcurrant, spice, floral	4–7 per cent	Medium
Mosaic	Blueberry, mango, passion fruit	10–14 per cent	High
Idaho 7	Mango, pink grapefruit, pine	9–12 per cent	High
Simcoe	Pine, grapefruit, passion fruit	11–15 per cent	High

From *Well Hopped! Hop Variety Brochure*, www.charlesfaram.co.uk

AUSTRALIAN HOPS

I was lucky enough to go to Australia in
2018 and put my status as a beer sommelier
to good use by helping to judge the Australian
International Beer Awards (AIBA). It involved
tasting 65 beers a day, for three days straight.
The glorious Aussie hop profile will be seared
in my brain forever. Australian hops are
known for their tropical fruits: think
pineapple, mango, apricot and peach.

HOP	FLAVOURS	ALPHA ACID	HOP INTENSITY
Vic Secret	Pineapple, pine	15–22 per cent	High
Enigma	White grape, redcurrant, rock melon	16–20 per cent	High
Galaxy	Passion fruit, peach, citrus	13–19 per cent	High
Topaz	Lychee, tropical fruit	16–20 per cent	High
Eclipse	Mandarin, citrus peel, pine	15–19 per cent	High

From From Hops from Australia (www.hops.com.au)

NEW ZEALAND HOPS

I find hops from New Zealand the most interesting of the lot. They can be musky and wine-like, or bring coconut and lime flavours. They are extremely varied. If you want to make a really unique pale ale, then New Zealand hops are the way to go. Their most famous hop would have to be Nelson Sauvin – known for its Sauvignon Blanc flavours (it's literally in the name), its wine-like characteristics are uncanny.

HOP	FLAVOURS	ALPHA ACID	HOP INTENSITY
Nelson Sauvin	White grape, gooseberry, grapefruit	10–13 per cent	High
Waimea	Orange, pine, resinous	16–19 per cent	Medium/high
Rakau	Apricot, passion fruit, pine	10–12 per cent	High
Pacific Gem	Blackberry, oak, pine	13–18 per cent	Medium
Green Bullet	Pine, plum, black pepper	10–13 per cent	Medium
Motueka	Lime, lemon, floral	5–8 per cent	High

From *Well Hopped! Hop Variety Brochure*, www.charlesfaram.co.uk

GERMAN AND CZECH REPUBLIC HOPS

Home to the famous quartet that are known as the noble hops: Saaz, Tettnanger, Spalt and Hallertauer Mittelfrüh. These hops in particular are known for their easy bittering, floral nose and spicy kick.

These classic noble hops are long associated with both pilsners as well as continental lagers.

HOP	FLAVOURS	ALPHA ACID	HOP INTENSITY
Saaz	Floral, herbal, spice	2–5 per cent	Low
Hallertauer Mittelfrüh	Herbal, floral, grassy	3–6 per cent	Low
Spalt	Tea, woodruff, spice	2–6 per cent	Low
Tettnanger	Herbal, floral, earthy	4–7 per cent	Low

From *Well Hopped! Hop Variety Brochure* and 'Hop, Flavours and Alpha Acid' from the Charles Faram Hop Brochure 2019 , www.charlesfaram.co.uk

SLOVENIAN HOPS

Slovenia's flourishing hop industry produces brewer favourites like Dana and, of course, their famous Styrian hops. Thanks to a very successful hop-breeding programme, the Slovenian Institute of Hop Research and Brewing, Slovenian hops are popular in English and Belgian beer styles.

HOP	FLAVOURS	ALPHA ACID	HOP INTENSITY
Dana	Floral, lemon, pine	9–13 per cent	Medium
Styrian Wolf	Lemon, lemon grass, mango	13–18 per cent	Medium
Atlas	Lime, floral, pine	5–9 per cent	Medium
Styrian Fox	Blackcurrant, lemon grass, marjoram	6–12 per cent	Medium

From *Well Hopped! Hop Variety Brochure*, www.charlesfaram.co.uk

EMERGING HOP GROWERS

There are many emerging hop growers all over the world – this year alone, I have seen hops from Spain, Portugal, South Africa and Argentina. They will certainly be developing over the next few years, and I for one am very excited to taste the terroir that comes from these emerging hop-growing regions.

Right: Hops growing in South Africa.

HOP FLOWERS & HOP PELLETS

Most hops are available to buy in at least two forms: flowers and pellets. Hop flowers are my premier hop form of choice on what we call the 'hot side' – that's during the brew process itself when everything is, well, hot. This, again, comes back to filterability. The hop flowers themselves act as a great filtration aid, and can be used to help clear the beer after boiling.

It is also possible to dry hop with flowers. This has been the case with dry hopping directly into cask beers for a long time. There is, however, a notable issue that becomes apparent the second you throw your hop flowers into a fermenter: they float! This reduces the overall contact between beer and hop, which leads to a muted, subtle flavour. As hop flowers and hop pellets are usually priced the same, you can get considerably more bang for your buck when dry hopping with pellets. Hop pellets tend to break down on contact with the beer – not completely, but in a way that releases a lot of juicy flavour. You will often see hop pellets referred to as 'T90 pellets'. T90 pellet hops have been milled and pressed. The interaction between beer and hop is generally much better when using T90 pellets, which makes them a more efficient choice when dry hopping straight into the fermenter.

BBC PELLET HOPS

The BBC stands for 'Boston Beer Company', as the type of hop was developed by them. In practical terms, the BBC hop pellet differs from the T90 in that it has a finer grind and has had more extraneous plant material removed. I've found that BBC hops mix better with the beer than T90 pellets, and have a stronger aroma. They tend to be sold at only a slightly higher price per kilogram than T90 pellets, I think they are worth the extra. Pictured is LUPOMAX™: this is a new concentrated pellet that is consistent, efficient, and optimized for hop flavour. LUPOMAX™ has less vegetative matter compared to regular hop pellets, so you get hop flavours that are bigger, bolder and brighter.

CRYO HOPS

Cryo hops cost at least twice as much as T90 pellets. But my oh my, they are beautiful. Cryo hops are frozen with liquid nitrogen, hence the word 'cryo', short for cryogenic. The lupulin glands (where essential oils and hop acids are found) are separated in the production process, resulting in cryo hops being a concentrated source for essential oils and bitterness. One of the main benefits of cryo hops is they give higher yields. Heavily double dry-hopped (DDH) beers suffer terribly from hop absorption – this means that the T90 hops you add to the fermenter for those big aromas absorb a lot of your beer, resulting in a lower volume of finished beer. Because cryo hops are so concentrated in flavour, you can use half the volume of cryo hops that you'd use of T90 hops. The hop aroma and flavour are simply outstanding.

In my opinion cryo hops are wasted in any area that is not the dry hop!

DRY HOPPING

Dry hopping is the process of adding hops straight into the fermenter in what we call the 'cold' side of brewing. There are many different ways to dry hop. Dry hopping directly into the fermenter is a relatively new beer technique (cask dry hopping aside), so there is a certain amount of variation in the ways different breweries and brewers choose to dry hop their beers.

The phrase DDH, or 'double dry hop', is one you see bandied about a lot these days. It literally means to dry hop the beer twice. Many brewers will tell you different things, but generally I have found the best times to dry hop are as follows.

1. AT HIGH KRAUSEN
'High krausen' typically occurs between 18 and 24 hours after the yeast has been pitched (adding yeast to your wort). You can physically see it! It is the thick, frothy, foamy layer on top of your fermenting beer. It relies on the interaction between hop oils and active yeast in a relatively newly discovered process known as biotransformation.

2. A FEW GRAVITY POINTS BEFORE THE END OF FERMENTATION
This is one of my favourite times to dry hop. You get amazing interaction between the hops and the beer.

3. AFTER FINAL GRAVITY HAS BEEN REACHED
Carbon dioxide (CO_2) can have a scrubbing effect on beer aroma, driving it off. Dry hopping after primary fermentation, when the majority of CO_2 has been produced by your yeast, can help to stop your precious beer aroma from floating away.

4. WHEN YOU CHILL THE BEER
You can add a dry hop just before chilling your beer. The convection currents brought on by the chilling process make for excellent mixing.

5. GENTLE CHILL
Gently chilling your beer to between 15–17°C (59–63°F) after primary fermentation is complete, holding the temperature steady, then dry hopping can give a great juicy aroma.

I know, I know, there are five dry hop methods here, not two. To double dry hop, any two of the above techniques should give you good results.

Above: Hops added to the fermenter.

THE BREWING PROCESS

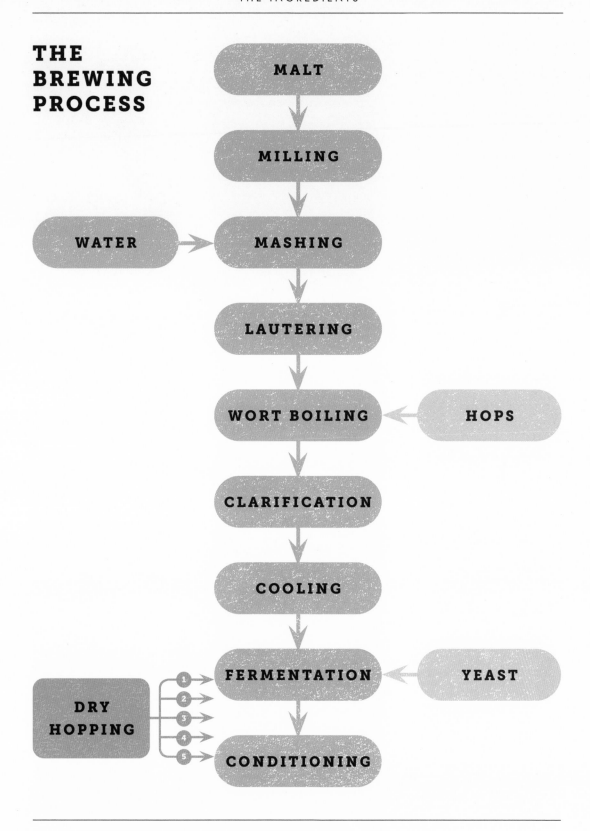

MALT

MILLING

WATER → MASHING

LAUTERING

WORT BOILING ← HOPS

CLARIFICATION

COOLING

FERMENTATION ← YEAST

DRY HOPPING
1
2
3
4
5

CONDITIONING

YEAST

Yeast is the fungus that makes beer possible. Yeast consumes sugars and produces alcohol and CO_2 as a consequence. It's the simplest of processes.

The species of yeast most prevalent in beer making is known as *Saccharomyces cerevisiae*. It is known as a top-fermenting ale yeast. This means that, during fermentation, the yeast likes to sit on top of the beer. This makes for easy viable yeast cropping, which is the removal of yeast from one batch of beer, which can then be either stored or reused for the next batch. It also likes to ferment warm, so the yeast prefers temperatures of around 20°C (68°F).

Lager is brewed with a different yeast, *Saccharomyces pastorianus*. Lager yeast differs from ale yeast in that it likes to be fermented cold, at around 12°C (54°F). It is known as bottom-fermenting, meaning it likes to sit at the bottom of your tank during fermentation.

One of the biggest tips I can give you when it comes to yeast, is BE KIND. Doing simple things like rehydrating dried yeast in clean water will make a big difference to your overall yeast health. Yeast does not like stress – who does? Your yeast can throw out all sorts of off flavours under stressful situations. So: don't let your yeast get too warm or too cold; avoid high pressures; make sure you don't underpitch (which is not adding enough yeast); and, if you're making a high-ABV beer and there is more sugar for your yeast to get through, add more yeast!

Your yeast is a living organism. Treat it well, and it will make you tasty beer.

Below: Jaega checks the temperature of the fermenting mash.

2

THE MICRO-ORGANISMS OF THE WILD BREWER

WILD YEAST AND BREWER'S YEAST

As complex as fermentation can sometimes seem, it is, in fact, quite straightforward. I used to feel quite daunted by phrases like 'spontaneous fermentation', but now I know there was no need. As brewers, we create the best environment we can to allow our chosen microorganisms to thrive. Sometimes we choose the yeast and bacteria that we think will make the best beer, and sometimes it's our environment that does the choosing, but we still control the setting. Even if the choice we make is to have no control whatsoever, for example, to attempt a completely open-top spontaneous fermentation in the middle of a farmhouse in Belgium, it's still a choice we've made – and we can expect a wild, untamed beer as a consequence.

As a professional brewer, it's just no good for me to make a delicious lactic acid sour when I was trying to make a pale ale. It's completely useless. If a customer was expecting a tasty pale ale, nothing would persuade them that this delicious lactic-soured beer was anything but an infection. My point is that intent is important. One of the most important lessons you will learn as a brewer is that good hygiene is central to making the beer you intend to make. Size doesn't matter – the same rules apply on a small scale as they do on a large scale. Clean, clean and clean some more.

Now that the inevitable cleanliness lecture is out of the way, let's break down the basics of different types of fermentation. The fermentation of beer can be split roughly into three areas: inoculated brewing, mixed fermentation and spontaneous fermentation.

Inoculated brewing
Inoculated brewing involves creating beer that is brewed in a controlled manner and inoculated with your chosen brewer's yeast, be that *Saccharomyces cerevisiae* or *Saccharomyces pastoranius* (for lagers). We're talking normal pale ales, lagers, IPAs and stouts – in other words, the majority of beers on the market. You can also inoculate your beer with bacteria or with *Brettanomyces* yeasts. The main caveat of inoculated brews is that the brewer has chosen the organisms to ferment and, in all likelihood, sour their beer. So beers like kettle sours also fall under this category: the brewer will have chosen the bacteria type and strain to sour their beer. There's more on kettle sours on page 120.

Mixed fermentation
Mixed fermentation tends to involve an inoculated fermentation (for example, using brewer's yeast in primary fermentation), but then the introduction of what I'll call a 'wild' environment. By that, I mean an environment where you don't have primary control over the yeasts or bacteria present. Brewing a stout,

Above: Fermentation in brewing.

then ageing your beer in a wooden barrel is a good example of mixed fermentation.

Spontaneous fermentation

Spontaneous fermentation occurs when an uncontrolled or wild environment is present throughout the entire fermentation process. This is probably the most unpredictable of all of the brewing techniques. The beers brewed using this technique are, quite simply, the products of their environment, and it's the terroir of that particular environment that makes a spontaneously fermented beer so unique. Wild yeast and bacteria are everywhere: in the air around us, nestled into the wood of a brewer's barrel, and in the rafters of the barn where the beer is brewed. Differing beer styles have developed partly because of the microbiological make-up of the organisms fermenting and souring beer in a particular region, and this is more prevalent when fermenting spontaneously than with any other method.

The reason why some areas in Belgium have become superb places to spontaneously ferment beer is no accident. It's down to centuries of conditioning: centuries of breweries brewing in a fairly small space, discarding the bad batches and only continuing to brew the carefully selected tastier batches. This slow conditioning has changed whole regions, as the continued brewing of particular batches has encouraged the growth of the relevant bacteria and wild yeast in the surrounding area, making certain parts of Belgium some of the best places in the world to produce these styles of spontaneously fermented beer.

I would argue that spontaneous fermentation is the least controllable area of beer making. You may make the finest nectar known to humankind – or you may end up with pigs' swill. What we are going to do, though, is shift the balance in the 'nectar of the gods' direction.

Taxonomy

Before we get into the details, it's handy to know how we categorise different organisms. You will often see terms like *Lactobacillus* or *Brettanomyces*, sometimes written in italics, sometimes not. What does all this mean? Some will be bacteria and other types of yeast. They will behave differently, feed differently, respire differently and reproduce differently, but – most importantly – they will also bring wildly different characteristics to your brew, and will require different environments in order to perform at their best.

So, let's start at the beginning...

Different organisms can be classified in a field known as taxonomy. It's a way of organising what's around us into groups. The organisms are grouped together according to their similarities, and separated according to their differences.

The term genus is used to categorise organisms that are similar. Specifically, a genus groups together closely related species. Genus names also tend to be written in Latin, hence the difficult pronunciation. A genus is always in italics (or underlined if writing by hand), with the first letter capitalised.

Lactobacillus, for example, is the genus. It currently contains over 180 different species of *Lactobacillus* bacteria. This is important to note, because in beer, you frequently hear about beer being produced with *Lactobacillus*. *Lactobacillus* what? Every single species of *Lactobacillus* will have its own flavour, produce different by-products, and have its own unique identity.

A species has two words in its name. The first is the genus, i.e. *Lactobacillus*. The second is its common name which is written in lower-case italics – for example, *Lactobacillus brevis*. Now that's clear, let's get into the nitty gritty.

LACTOBACILLUS

Lactobacillus is a group of gram-positive rod-shaped bacteria. The species of *Lactobacillus* is capable of fermenting both when there is oxygen and when there isn't (generally, reduced oxygen levels are preferred).

To a certain extent, *Lactobacillus* bacteria can be seen as quite similar to brewer's yeast, in that they consume sugar and produce CO_2, but instead of producing ethanol, they produce lactic acid. *Lactobacillus* bacteria like to operate at a warmer temperature: rather than the generally accepted 20°C (68°F) preferred by *Saccharomyces cerevisiae*, *Lactobacillus* enjoys a sweltering 37°C (98°F). *Lactobacillus* bacteria are generally known as being fast acting, especially in comparison to other lactic acid-producing bacteria, such as the *Pediococcus* species – we are talking days to weeks, rather than months.

This species is most commonly found in yogurt and other soured dairy (lassi, anyone?). It's also found in the human digestive system, the urinary system and in the vagina.

In order to find the brewing styles that rely on *Lactobacillus* bacteria as the primary souring method of choice, we need to look towards the towering brewing juggernaut that is Germany. Berliner Weisse and *gose* beers are friends of *Lactobacillus*. They are both styles with low to moderate ABV and low bitterness, and perfectly show off the best of lactic acid's attributes. Lactic acid is a fairly soft, tangy acid and can have creamy overtones. It is not what one would describe as particularly complex. While this simplicity is undesirable for more complex sour beer styles, it can be absolute perfection when brewed with or paired with fruit, as is so often the case with the Berliner Weisse. For how to brew a *gose* or Berliner Weisse, see page 64.

Some species of *Lactobacillus* will consume sugar and produce only lactic acid (*Lactobacillus delbrueckii*, for example). Plain and simple. These are known as homofermentative. But others, such as *Lactobacillus brevis,* will produce several other by-products in addition to lactic acid, including CO_2, acetic acid, diacetyl and even ethanol. These are known as heterofermentative.

Most malt is laden with *Lactobacillus* bacteria. In fact, *Lactobacillus* bacteria are the primary target when brewers speak of the antibacterial nature of hops. Hops play an important role in keeping bacteria in check. So, if you would like to sour your brew with *Lactobacillus* bacteria, remember that hops have the power to destroy the very bacteria you are trying to grow. When brewing these styles, keep your hop additions to a minimum. Although it is true that different species of *Lactobacillus* have different hop tolerances, in general I would recommend no higher than 7 IBU (International Bitterness Units) when brewing your beer to allow for the general hop sensitivity of *Lactobacillus* bacteria.

High levels of ethanol or lactic acid will also inhibit the growth of *Lactobacillus* bacteria, so you will reach a point where your beer will simply sour no more, inhibited by the very lactic acid it has produced. Most *Lactobacillus* bacteria preferred by brewers will comfortably get your beer to a pH of 3.4–3.6.

In the world of clean brewing, *Lactobacillus* bacteria are spoilage organisms. In this, the world of funk, they are your friends.

TYPES OF *LACTOBACILLUS*

Found in: Berliner Weisse, *gose*

LACTOBACILLUS DELBRUECKII

ABOUT ME
Common species in beer making. Homofermentative and hop sensitive.

WHEN TO PITCH
Primary fermentation, secondary fermentation or in longer-term beer storage.

LACTOBACILLUS PLANTARUM

ABOUT ME
Quick souring and hop sensitive. Ideal temperature 25–27°C (77–81°F). Can grow in a low-pH environment.

WHEN TO PITCH
Primary fermentation, secondary fermentation or in longer-term beer storage

LACTOBACILLUS BREVIS

ABOUT ME
Heterofermentative. Can produce a number of different compounds, including – but not limited to – lactic acid, ethanol, acetic acid and CO_2. Some are capable of fermenting starch and dextrins (see page 70). Ideal temperature around 30°C (86°F). Can tolerate some hopping. Common in beer spoilage.

WHEN TO PITCH
Primary fermentation, secondary fermentation or in longer-term beer storage.

LACTOBACILLUS BUCHNERI

ABOUT ME
Heterofermentative. Can produce a number of different compounds, including – but not limited to – lactic acid, ethanol, acetic acid and CO_2. Can produce moderate acidity.

WHEN TO PITCH
Primary fermentation, secondary fermentation or in longer-term beer storage.

PEDIOCOCCUS

The species of *Pediococcus* are lactic acid-producing gram-positive bacteria. They are homofermentative in nature and mainly produce lactic acid, with no CO_2. They are famous for playing a major role in the production of sauerkraut.

One of the main attributes to note when working with *Pediococcus* bacteria is that they take ages – they are as slow at producing lactic acid as *Lactobacillus* bacteria are fast. This lengthy wait time can allow the main brewer's yeast to crack on with its primary fermentation long before a significant amount of lactic acid has been produced, which advantageously prevents the brewer's yeast from fermenting in a stressful low-pH environment. This slow pace lends itself perfectly to longer-term production, so is great for barrel ageing.

Pediococcus bacteria tend to be more hop resilient than their fellow lactic acid-producing companion species *Lactobacillus* bacteria, although they are similar in that neither species likes high levels of alcohol. *Pediococcus* bacteria can handle low levels of oxygen, but are capable of producing anaerobically.

When *Pediococcus* bacteria take hold, the inexperienced brewer might be alarmed: the long, thick, slimy tentacles that form are off-putting, to say the least. But when you're brewing wild beers, this is, in fact, a cause for celebration: a physical sign that you have successfully produced a *Pediococcus* bacterial infection. It is most often described as 'ropey' in appearance and generally likes to sit near the top of your brew. I've always thought it looks like thick, pale, slimy oil. These 'ropey' tentacles are known as exopolysaccharides, and are made up of carbohydrates, proteins and acid. Be warned, though: not all species of *Pediococcus* will produce this ropey effect.

One of the main disadvantages of *Pediococcus* bacteria is the sheer amount of diacetyl they produce as a by-product. Unlike brewer's yeast, which, towards the end of fermentation, breaks down the diacetyl into constituents less damaging to your flavour profile, with *Pediococcus* bacteria, there is no such luck. The diacetyl will stick around, its butterscotch flavour profile single-handedly ruining your brew. However, there is hope. The addition of *Brettanomyces* yeast will save the day, eliminate diacetyl and also break down and ferment the ropey exopolysaccharides.

In essence, souring a beer with only *Pediococcus* bacteria is a bad idea. Pair them with the right yeast, though, and it can be glorious.

Pediococcus bacteria are easily capable of reaching a pH of 3, so have the power to produce some seriously tart beer.

TYPES OF *PEDIOCOCCUS*

Found in: lambic, Berliner Weisse

PEDIOCOCCUS DAMNOSUS

ABOUT ME

Modestly hop tolerant, and can cope with oxygen, i.e. aerobic. Produces diacetyl as a by-product. Has generally high alcohol tolerance (up to 12 per cent). Optimum temperature 22–25°C (72–77°F). Struggles to reproduce at a pH of below 3.4.

WHEN TO PITCH

Primary fermentation, secondary fermentation or in longer-term beer storage. Use as part of a mixed culture to offset the large amounts of diacetyl produced.

PEDIOCOCCUS PARVULUS

ABOUT ME

Common *Pediococcus* species found in wine making. Reproduces at a higher pH and lower temperatures than *Pediococcus damnosus*. Can cause 'ropiness'.

WHEN TO PITCH

Secondary fermentation or in longer-term beer storage.

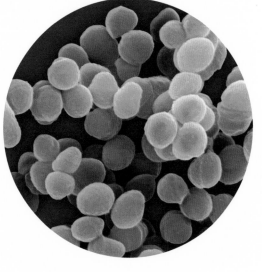

ACETOBACTER

In the presence of ethanol and oxygen, *Acetobacter* bacteria produce acetic acid, more commonly known as vinegar. *Acetobacter* bacteria are generally airborne, and can be found all over the world. Leave your pint unguarded for a few days and of all the spoilage organisms, *Acetobacter* bacteria will probably make a meal of it first.

Acetobacter commonly rears its ugly head at the end of the life of a cask of beer. With every pint that's poured, air gets drawn into the cask, and the airborne *Acetobacter* bacteria will inevitably be drawn in with it. This combination of an oxygen-rich environment and ethanol is like Christmas for *Acetobacter* bacteria. At cellar temperature, spoilage can occur in a matter of weeks, hence the famously short shelf life of the British institution that is cask beer. *Acetobacter* bacteria will grow rapidly at 25–30°C (77–86°F), so if your cellar is too warm, spoilage can occur in a matter of days. If you catch a whiff of vinegar in a pint of cask beer in the pub, which unfortunately is all too common, send it straight back. It will be riddled with *Acetobacter* bacteria. There are times for British politeness, and this is not one of them.

Acetic acid is distinctive: it is tangy, sharp and has the power to instantly make your body recoil at a beer. On the scale of sour acids, I would say that acetic acid is perceived as the most 'sour', if that makes any sense at all! It can be a harsh, unpleasant, wrinkle-up-your-nose kind of tangy sour.

In the company of some *Brettanomyces* yeasts, acetic acid and ethanol can be converted into ethyl acetate, which, when present in small quantities, can give a flavour of pear drops. In bigger quantities, though, ethyl acetate has the distinct unpleasantness of nail varnish remover. Sounds delicious. For more information on ethyl acetate, see page 176.

I feel like I'm being quite negative about *Acetobacter* bacteria and its product, acetic acid. As a brewer, its presence usually fills me with fear and shame, as it's generally a strong sign of a dirty bar or a container you really should have cleaned sooner. Using it successfully in a beer is, in my opinion, nothing short of masterful.

In small quantities, this can be quite beautiful. Its highly distinctive flavour is the backbone of the Flanders red: try it once and I promise you, you won't forget it. It is also present, to a lesser extent, in lambic beers. When it is used delicately, it adds a really stunning complexity.

I wouldn't add *Acetobacter* bacteria in with your primary fermentation. Even though this bacteria is hop tolerant, it requires a steady supply of oxygen to do its business (aka acetic acid production). The CO_2 produced by brewer's yeast will restrict its activity. If you want to end up with fairly low levels of acetic acid in your brew, add a small amount of unpasteurised vinegar when pitching your other wild microorganisms. The unpasteurised vinegar will contain *Acetobacter* bacteria.

If you wanted to cheat and get that acetic acid flavour without any of the work (or risk), buy some malt vinegar and blend it into your beer prior to packaging. This method is considered utter sacrilege by most brewers, but I'm a big believer in having one's arsenal fully loaded.

TYPES OF *ACETOBACTER*

Found in: Flanders red, lambic, spoiled cask beer

ACETOBACTER ACETI

ABOUT ME
Converts ethanol into acetic acid in the presence of oxygen. Rapid growth between at 25–30°C (77–86°F).

WHEN TO PITCH
After primary fermentation, in small quantities with the rest of your secondary fermentation culture.

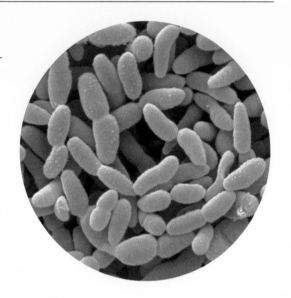

BRETTANOMYCES

In the beer world, it's common to hear the phrase 'Bretted beer', or hear people referring to a beer containing 'Brett'. No, 'Brett' is not the name of your cool new American friend – they are, in fact, referring to the *Brettanomyces* genus, which is a type of yeast. Famous for their use in lambics, Flanders reds and gueuze, *Brettanomyces* yeasts are known for their funky, wild, untamed flavours.

Literally meaning 'British fungus,' *Brettanomyces* yeasts are, in fact, found all over the world. They were first discovered at the turn of the twentieth century, when scientists at both Guinness and the New Carlsberg Brewery noticed a slow secondary fermentation happening in English cask ales. This sluggish secondary fermentation was the work of *Brettanomyces* yeasts.

When brewers talk of 'wild yeast' they are generally speaking of the *Brettanomyces* species. These yeasts are found on fruit skins, on trees, blowing around in the wind and, in all likelihood, in your house. They would have been commonplace in beer before the introduction of modern sanitation, with each region – each brewery – having their own unique yeast strains infecting their beer, adding an unknown terroir to their brew.

Brettanomyces yeasts are what we call 'super attenuating'. That means that when all else has been fermented, *Brettanomyces* yeasts will ferment some more. They are capable of nearly 100 per cent attenuation. Unlike regular brewer's yeast, *Brettanomyces* species are capable of fermenting dextrins. (Dextrins are a group of carbohydrates that have low molecular weight and are generally far too complex for brewer's yeast to be able to ferment.)

The wide range of flavours possible from *Brettanomyces* yeasts is astonishing. Different species of *Brettanomyces* can impact your brew in very different ways. The genus is incredibly diverse, with flavours ranging from the funkiness of horse and barnyard, to the more effervescent pineapple (or, dare I say it, the dreaded faecal flavour). There are five species in the *Brettanomyces* genus, but the two most common used in brewing are *Brettanomyces anomalus* and *Brettanomyces bruxellensis*. Even within these two species there is huge variety. Brewer's yeast is similar in this way: it is capable of producing wheat beers, saisons and pale ales – all with very different flavours. Within one specific species of *Brettanomyces* there are various strains, each of which can offer huge variety in terms of both flavour and aroma.

A common mistake made by brewers and drinkers alike is to associate *Brettanomyces* with sourness. It's important to note that, while the species of *Brettanomyces* will add many different flavours, among them mousey, barnyard and fruity flavours, acids are not generally produced (unless there is an extreme excess of oxygen, in which case they can produce acetic acid). So *Brettanomyces* yeasts are not generally seen as souring organisms. It's the combination of other organisms, such as *Pediococcus* or *Lactobacillus* bacteria, that produces those acids. This important distinction helps you to separate the flavours borne from the *Brettanomyces* yeasts from those generally borne from sour-producing bacteria.

Brettanomyces yeasts can add a complexity and uniqueness to your brew that is simply unrivalled. They can also be unpredictable – but that's all part of the joy of brewing with them! They are generally slow fermenters – much slower than most brewer's yeast – think months rather than weeks. They prefer to ferment in lower-pH environments and will work well in mixed cultures. Although there are few commercial examples in existence, 100 per cent *Brettanomyces* yeast ferments are totally possible. Be adventurous.

There is a strong association between *Brettanomyces* yeasts and barrel-ageing beer. If you store your beer in oak, it will probably pick up some of this yeast. The genus of *Brettanomyces* contains five recognised species: *Brettanomyces anomalus*, *Brettanomyces bruxellensis*, *Brettanomyces custersianus*, *Brettanomyces nanus* and *Brettanomyces naardenensis*. The two species outlined over the page are commonly found in barrel-aged beer and wine production. The third, *Brettanomyces custersians*, has potential, but limited commercial usage. Perfect for an experiment!

TYPES OF *BRETTANOMYCES*

Found in: Flanders red, lambic, spoiled cask beer

BRETTANOMYCES ANOMALUS

(sometimes called *Brettanomyces claussenii*)*

ABOUT ME

Common species used in brewing. Also found in cider production. Associated with pineapple and barnyard funk.

WHEN TO PITCH

With brewer's yeast, after primary fermentation, or on its own. Make sure yeast is healthy when pitching after primary fermentation, as simple sugars and oxygen are scarce. This yeast loses viability at 36°C (97°F).

BRETTANOMYCES CUSTERSIANUS

ABOUT ME

Has had limited commercial use. Anecdotal evidence suggests this strain exhibits little in the way of the funky barnyard flavours described above and is instead very fruity, with flavours of peach, pineapple and mango.

WHEN TO PITCH

With so little available evidence, it's difficult to say. My instinct would be to follow the pitching instructions of the more established beer strains *Brettanomyces anomalus* and *Brettanomyces bruxellensis*. Have fun!

* Synonyms are common in the world of *Brettanomyces* yeasts.
  Be prepared – it can cause confusion!

BRETTANOMYCES BRUXELLENSIS

(sometimes called *Brettanomyces lambicus*)*

ABOUT ME

Common species used in brewing. A key component of several prominent Belgian styles, such as lambics, Flanders reds and gueuze. Associated with horsey, barnyard, earthy flavours. Commonly associated with wine spoilage. Frequently detected in red wines that have been barrel-aged and have high pH and low sulphur dioxide levels.

WHEN TO PITCH

With brewer's yeast, after primary fermentation, or on its own. Make sure yeast is healthy when pitching after primary fermentation, as simple sugars and oxygen are scarce. This yeast loses viability at 36°C (97°F).

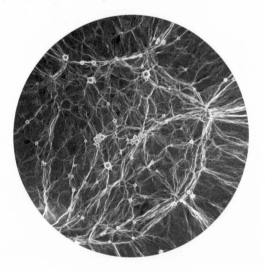

3

BARREL AGEING

THE BARREL

The wooden barrel or cask is a cylindrical container
made up of wooden staves which are bound together
with hoops of metal. It is narrower at the edges with
a wider, fuller belly in the middle. It's a hollow container,
which has been used for the storage and transport
of goods for centuries. Nowadays, however,
it is famous for its use in the food industry.

There are many examples of wooden containers stretching as far back as ancient Mesopotamia. Herodotus, the ancient Greek historian, mentions the use of wooden barrels in his writings. The barrels were said to be made of palm wood and were used to transport Armenian wine to Babylon, one of Mesopotamia's key kingdoms.

The most popular container choice in the ancient world, however, was the amphora. An amphora is a hardened clay pot with handles on either side. You would recognise one instantly, I'm sure. They are seen in every TV programme or movie depicting ancient Rome, the Egyptians or pretty much any ancient civilisation.

Although the wooden barrel is mentioned in the texts of these ancient civilisations, it is in fact the Celts of Northern Europe who are credited with its invention. The beginnings of the barrel as we know it can be dated to some time between 500 and 1000 BCE. The Iron Age Celts had managed to combine their woodwork and, most crucially, their iron-working skills. Barrels could hold large volumes, were easy to move around due to their propensity to roll, and could transport a wide variety of liquid and dry goods. Compared to the amphora, which was fragile and difficult to take with you on long

distances, the wooden barrel must have been a revelation.

The Romans managed to appropriate the wooden barrel technology and, with their vast network, spread barrel-making knowhow across their many trade roots. The barrel remained the dominant form of transport container for over 2,000 years. It wasn't until the development of the pallet, which was relatively recent, that barrels fell out of favour as the main type of transport container.

Wooden barrels were once used to transport all sorts of goods – from golden coins to fish, oil and tobacco. It was discovered fairly early on that when you placed perishable goods like wine or ale in a wooden barrel, the drink would take on some of the flavour of the wood – often for the better. This meant that the type of wood used was important. Although I'm sure lots of different types of wood were tried for barrel-making over the centuries, oak became the dominant material. It was pliable, yet strong and durable. It was easy to bend and easy to toast, which meant you could make oak barrels fairly quickly. Oak was also abundant: Europe was covered with the stuff. But, most importantly of all, due to its tight grain nature, it was watertight.

It was this connection to the drinks industry that saved the wooden barrel from extinction.

In the twentieth century, transport was no longer the primary use of the wooden barrel. Tankers, metal drums, steel casks and the humble cardboard box had seen to that. The fundamental use of the wooden barrel had become the ageing of wine and spirits.

Legislation was passed in Kentucky, USA, that ensured all bourbon whiskey was matured in brand new oak barrels, giving barrel makers – or coopers, as they are known – a job to do. Used bourbon barrels from the US whiskey industry are sought-after – they tend to end up with Scottish whisky and Irish whiskey producers. Rum producers are also known to love a bourbon barrel, as do several notable apple brandy producers. Winemakers today are also big users of brand new wooden barrels. Meanwhile, barrels that have previously been used for port, sherry and cognac often make their way into the whisky industry.

The beer industry are avid users of wooden barrels too. These versatile containers are used not only to mature beer, but to ferment it as well. But it's important to note that they do come with increased complexities, especially when compared to brewing in stainless steel.

Oak barrels can provide a certain amount of exchange with the outside world. It is possible that using wooden barrels can cause oxidation of your beer and the evaporation of your beer, but both of these processes do happen very slowly. I often say, 'oxygen is the enemy' after beer is fermented, and in most cases when working with clean beer, that is true. But when working with wooden barrels, that permeation of oxygen through the hard oak is helpful, as it allows *Brettanomyces* yeasts to thrive in that environment. In all likelihood, the *Brettanomyces* yeasts are absorbing the slowly penetrating oxygen before significant oxidation of the beer even has a chance to occur.

Some species of *Brettanomyces* yeasts are known to feed off the oak itself, breaking down even wood sugars. They can also penetrate the oak itself, making them extremely difficult to remove once established. The complex relationship between the *Brettanomyces* species and oak is not fully understood: the yeasts have even been found in brand-new, unused oak barrels. Think of it like this: when working with oak barrels, *Brettanomyces* yeasts are largely to be expected.

You may have noticed that oak gets the majority of the attention when it comes to barrel ageing. When it comes to wine, spirits and, as a consequence, beer as well, oak is the leading material used to make barrels. Other woods are used, such as chestnut, but they are much harder to get hold of.

Left: A cooper bounding the woods.

BEER AND OAK

Oak can add a wide variety of different flavours to beer. If you are lucky enough to get your hands on an unused oak barrel, the natural oaky flavour is easier to detect. Each time you use a barrel, more of the oak flavour is removed from the barrel and transferred into your beer. The flavour of first-use barrels can be overwhelming and intense. If you do choose to age your beer in a brand-new barrel, consider reducing the length of time your beer will be in contact with the wood.

There are five flavours generally associated with oak itself, and these are the ones you should be looking out for. They are:

- **VANILLA**
- **COCONUT**
- **CARAMEL OR BUTTER**
- **CLOVE AND SPICE**
- **SMOKE**

Barrels used in the beer industry tend to come from the cellars of wine and spirit industries, with brewers often getting their hungry mitts on them after their second or third use. By the time the brewer works with a barrel, it's probably several years old, and the assertive flavours associated with the oak will have become far weaker.

When choosing a barrel, there are five things you need to consider:

- **WOOD TYPE**
- **AGE**
- **PREVIOUS CONTENTS**
- **TOAST**
- **VOLUME**

Each of these characteristics will have an effect on the flavour a barrel gives to your beer. How the barrel staves were cut and dried, their degree of toast at manufacture (see page 82) and their place of origin will all have an impact. I like to think of each barrel as an individual. They will each have their own history, their own experiences and – very importantly – their own ecosystem contained within. The same beer can taste very different from two different barrels, just like the same recipe can taste very different when brewed by two different breweries. There are myriad factors involved, and some of them are not controllable by you. This is why it is important to consider blending batches if you want to achieve excellent barrel-aged beers with any consistency. Blending batches has been one of the keys to the success of the Belgian wild beers. The fact that they bring out superb beer year after year is testament to this technique.

TYPES OF OAK

We've established that oak is the primary wood used to make barrels, but oak barrels can be organised even further by their places of origin. We're going to look at oak from three main locations: America, France and Hungary (although there are many more). The home of an oak barrel and the resulting flavours it imparts on your wine, whisky or beer has been the subject of much debate. Preference for each is, of course, a matter of personal taste. I've outlined a handy guide that shows some of the different flavours and characteristics you can expect from each oak source.

AMERICAN OAK
- strong vanilla
- toasted coconut
- dill
- cocoa
- caramel

FRENCH OAK
- subtle vanilla
- cloves
- cedar
- nutmeg
- allspice

HUNGARIAN OAK
- mellow vanilla
- cinnamon
- toffee
- butterscotch

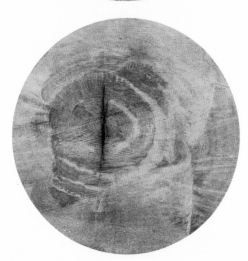

TOAST LEVELS

In the barrel-making process, in order to curve the hard oak into shape, the cooper toasts the barrel, either in an oven or with an open flame.

Different levels of toast will add different flavours to your beer. A lighter toast gives hints of vanilla, clove and caramel. A medium toast gives elements of vanilla, coffee and nuts. A heavy toast will give flavours of charcoal, coffee and nutmeg.

As a general rule of thumb, a lighter toast tends to suit lighter beers, such as *saisons*. For those Imperial stouts, a heavy-toasted barrel would be better suited.

There is a lot to take into account, right? What with the wood type, the oak type, the toast level and the barrel's previous content, there's potentially a lot of flavours milling around. I always like to say, when dealing with so much information that it's borderline overwhelming, one should simplify. Your most helpful tool here is your nose. Sniff, sniff, then sniff some more! Have a sniff of your wood. Start with short, sharp sniffs for your lighter, more delicate aromatics, then long, heavy sniffs, like you've never sniffed anything so hard in your life, for your more intense, heavier aromatics. Tailoring beer recipes to suit the type of barrel you have can be very worthwhile, and is much easier than doing things the other way round.

Above: A cooper toasting the barrel.

LIGHT TOAST	MEDIUM TOAST	HEAVY TOAST

BARREL AGEING AT HOME

Barrel ageing at home can be quite a challenge, but I can recommend a few easy ways to have a go!

BUY SOME SMALL BARRELS

You can buy small oak barrels for use at home. They come in a variety of sizes to suit different homebrew setups. This route is the most expensive, but barrels can be a real long-term investment if you treat them properly. You will need a minimum of two barrels in order to make beers like the *gueuze* or to blend lambic batches. Caring for your barrel is the same on a small scale as it is on a large one (see page 152). There is one major difference, however, that should be noted. Smaller homebrew-size barrels have thinner staves and a high surface-to-volume ratio. This means that your beer will potentially both oxidate and evaporate faster than it would in a larger barrel. Also, bear in mind that a brand new 10-litre oak barrel will have all of the challenges of any larger brand new barrel. The oak flavour will be intense! You will probably only want to put your beer in a new oak barrel for a short period of time. I would advise filling your barrel 2–3 times with 'clean' beer well suited to stronger oak characteristics before you consider adding souring micro-organisms.

For instructions on how to fill a barrel, see page 86.

USE WOOD CHIPS

Some brewers would omit this as an option, I'm sure, but I am not one of them! I know that not everyone has the money to buy several barrels for a home barrel-ageing

programme. I think it's important to recognise what wood chips can do for your brew, and also to consider the limitations of this method rather than just dismissing it out of hand. This is about using wood chips to improve your beer, combining the oak flavours and the flavour of your beer to make a better, more nuanced brew than you had before. Add your oak chips during secondary fermentation. As always, taste, taste, then taste again. It's vital to keep tasting your beer to make sure you don't go overboard with the oak flavour. Vanilla is a yes; woody flavours are definitely a no. As wood chips are very small, the surface area is very high. You can achieve quite an intense woody flavour in a matter of weeks, and it's easy to go overboard. So if you do choose to use wood chips, make sure you taste your beer every 1–2 days of ageing, so you hit that sweet spot. The last thing you would want to do after all that brewing effort is to go overboard and end up with a beer that tastes like you're chewing a table leg. If this does happen, you have no choice but to blend your beer with other batches to tone it down. Brewers often complain that the flavour from wood chips is comparatively 'one note' when compared to using larger wood pieces like wooden staves or spirals (see below).

WOOD PIECES

Just as you can source different barrels, you can also source different kinds of oak pieces, including cubes, spirals, chunks or staves. The larger the pieces of barrel you can find, the closer you can get to achieving the flavour of authentic barrel ageing. Large oak pieces offer what chips cannot: the slow release of flavour into your beer. A good place to start is to use 1.5g wood cubes per litre for a period of at least a month. This will give you a fairly mild flavour that can be built up if required. You can also find oak pieces from barrels that

once contained rum or whisky, for example. While getting hold of wood from old barrels is preferable, it is also possible to pre-soak your wood pieces in the wine or spirit of your choice. If you choose to do this, I would advise soaking for three days for most spirits, and the same for wine – but be cautious to avoid oxygenation of your wine if possible. You don't want to produce vinegar here!

FILL A BARREL WITH FRIENDS

If you are a member of a homebrew club, you could try to persuade your brewing buddies to club together and fill a brewer's barrel. As a project, it can be a fair amount of fun! First, you will need a barrel. Try local distilleries or wineries, or give a cooperage a call. I work with Speyside Cooperage in Scotland, who handle all my barrel-related needs. Secondly, you need somewhere to store a barrel long term. This depends on the set-up of your homebrew club: it may or may not be possible. Bear in mind that a barrel is fairly heavy and likely to stay in the same position for several years. The third thing you need is a group of homebrewers! For a 220-litre barrel, you need about 12 homebrewers. A standard homebrewing batch is about 23 litres, but minus wastage, you can assume you'll get about 18 litres per person. If each of you makes approximately the same recipe at the same time (see the Recipes chapter for ideas), then you can all fill the barrel on the same day. Another plus: packaging a barrel is also considerably easier with 12 people!

4

GET FRUITY

FRUIT BEERS

These are one of my favourite beer styles to drink. When a brewer gets it right, a fruit beer can be glorious: like the heavens opening, angels singing. But when a brewer gets it wrong, it can be beyond disappointing. All that hard work and effort just for someone to say: 'They used mango? Really?! I couldn't even taste it!'

Fruit beers have, for some reason or another, long been associated with women. You might hear a bartender suggesting 'a fruit beer for the lady'. It is a cause of irritation for me, and probably many other women, too. In my experience, it just isn't true.

When you're dealing with a customer that announces: 'I don't like beer, but I love fruit ciders,' introducing them to a fruity Berliner Weisse is often an easy win. The pH levels of cider and that of a light sour are similar, so the distance to travel between the two drinks is not that great. But people do surprise you. More than once, I've seen the person that announces they 'don't like beer' end up clutching a 10 per cent Russian Imperial stout – definitely not a beer usually associated with beginners.

The first time I brewed with fruit was problematic. In fact, not just problematic – it was explosive. Literally. Most fruits are laden with simple sugars, normally fructose and glucose. Additionally there are usually some more complex sugars present. The rest of your fruit is made up of pectin, tannins, aroma compounds and vegetative matter, all in various quantities, depending on the fruit you're working with. It's very important to remember that when you add fruit to your brew, you add sugar. You need to give your chosen microorganisms ample opportunity to feast on your fruit sugars, either in primary or secondary fermentation. If not, you'll end up with an explosive mess – as I found out to my ceiling's detriment. When you bottle beer at home, the beer will usually contain residual yeast. This yeast will continue to consume your unchecked fruit sugar in the bottle, producing more CO_2 in a finite space. This increases the pressure inside the container, and eventually leads to exploding bottles. No one needs that! These pitfalls are so avoidable. Following a few simple rules will help you get it right, every time.

The first thing you have to decide is the type of fruit you want to brew with. It sounds straightforward, but there is usually a whole plethora of different factors you have to take into account before you can begin your brew. What type of beer do you want to brew? Does it really need a fruit addition, and, if it does, have you left enough space in the recipe development and the beer's flavour profile to really let that fruit shine? Brewing with fruit, especially real fruit (not essences), can be one of the most complex, challenging and rewarding brewing experiences. But be warned: this is not for the faint-hearted! I would certainly recommend being able to brew cleanly, with no 'off' flavours in your brew, before you even attempt this. But this is not a book for the unadventurous, so here goes...

FRUIT TYPES

You can buy fruit in a variety of different formats. Depending on what you want to achieve, each has its advantages and disadvantages.

FRESH FRUIT

The epitome of fruity brewing. Brewing with fresh fruit has an authenticity, a wholesomeness. It's like comparing a sourdough bread to a sliced white loaf. Fresh fruit is high in flavour, cheap (when bought seasonally) and, whether it's picked from your own garden or bought from your local greengrocer, you know – or can easily find out – where it has come from.

However, brewing with fresh fruit is not all sunshine and daisies. The first time I brewed with fruit commercially was with fresh raspberries. I had been down to New Spitalfields market in East London the night before and

haggled for my fruit. New Spitalfields market is where London's fanciest restaurants buy their fruit and veg in the dead of night. Trading starts there at 11 p.m., but in reality many of the traders won't sell you a bean until they're fully set up at around 1 a.m. So I turned up at the brewery the next day with my raspberries, a food processor and a lot of determination. Once the raspberries had been crushed and whizzed, I added them to the brew at the end of the boil, feeling pretty chuffed. What I hadn't counted on were the seeds. Those damn raspberry seeds happened to be exactly the same size as the holes in the filter at the bottom of the kettle. So obviously, they blocked the kettle completely! I had to use every ounce of engineering skill I possess to free my raspberry beer from its seedy prison. Fate was cruel that day. My point: using fresh raspberries in a commercial brew can be impractical. It's important you use what's viable for your situation.

TOP TIP

It is important that you take a gravity reading before and after the addition of fruit. This will help you to calculate the final alcoholic content of your beer.

· · ·

RULE OF THUMB

Fresh active yeast will convert simple sugars in fruit into alcohol and CO_2.

· · ·

RULE OF THUMB

Bacteria is more likely to act on sugar before you see any significant response from the yeast when you add fruit to matured aged sour beer.

HOW MUCH FRUIT DO I ADD?

- **Blackberries:** 120–500g per litre
- **Blueberries:** 120–350g per litre
- **Cherries:** 120–500g per litre
- **Raspberries:** 30–375g per litre
- **Mango:** 50–120g per litre
- **Apricot:** 180–500g per litre

WHEN SHOULD I ADD IT?

Kettle, fermenter, secondary fermentation.

FROZEN FRUIT

Whether you're using fruit you've frozen yourself or fruit from a supermarket's frozen aisle, freezing can be a great way to work around the seasonality of fresh fruit.

With traditional freezing methods, i.e. if you put it in your own freezer, the water within the fruit freezes and expands, which will cause a rupture of the cell wall. Water is one of the few known substances whose density decreases upon a change of state – going from a liquid to a solid form. It's the reason why ice floats and icebergs exist. Most liquids shrink upon freezing, as the molecular structure becomes more tightly packed. Water follows this same shrinking pattern until it reaches 4°C (39°F), but below that, it slowly begins to expand until the freezing point is reached. When water freezes, it expands in volume by a massive 9 per cent (approximately).

Although this rupturing of the cell wall would be less appealing if you wanted to eat the fruit whole (no one wants to eat a wet, mushy strawberry), it can actually be advantageous to the brewing process. When the cell walls burst, a huge amount of the fruit flavour and colour is released. Because of this, using frozen fruit instead of fresh fruit can work well when making beer.

WHEN SHOULD I ADD IT?
Kettle, fermenter, secondary fermentation.

Above left: Cell in natural state.

Above right: Cell wall broken after freezing.

PULPS AND PURÉES

One of the most common questions I am asked when talking about fruit is: 'What's the difference between a pulp and a purée?' The answer: not a lot. The two words are often used interchangeably. In the grand scheme of things, a pulp and a purée are in fact very similar. However, there are differences that must be noted, albeit small ones.

A fruit pulp is the edible part of the fruit that has been pressed. Pulp has often had the membranes within the fruit crushed, releasing more juice. The final product contains the juice as well as the fibrous content of the fruit. It can, depending on the fruit you're working with, have a similar consistency to a marmalade.

A purée, on the other hand, is exactly that: fruit that has been puréed. So it should be smooth and contain no lumps.

Both pulps and purées are stabilised for storage in some way, whether that's pasteurisation, freezing or the addition of formic or sorbic acid. One of the major benefits of both fruit pulps and purées is that they retain the same flavour, aroma, taste and colour as the whole fruit, as well as its beneficial nutrients.

On a commercial scale, I love brewing with fruit purée. My only issue is the sheer amount of volume it adds to your brew. You have to take this into account. If you have a 20-litre brew, and you want to add 5 litres of purée, but your fermenter is only 23 litres... well...

Another thing to watch out for when buying fruit pulps or purées is their sugar content. Many small-scale, readily available purées are made for use in cocktails, and they have often had sugar added. Always check the ingredients to ensure that what you are buying is the fruit alone and nothing else.

WHEN SHOULD I ADD IT?
Kettle, fermenter, secondary fermentation.

JUICES AND CONCENTRATE

Freshly squeezed juice is delicious, but it does have its limitations. Untreated fresh juice has a short shelf life, which can limit its use in beer. If you do use freshly squeezed juice, whether you make it yourself or buy it, always taste it before adding it to your beer. You wouldn't want to ruin your beer by adding spoiled juice.

Widely available in supermarkets, however, are fresh juices that have had minimal heat treatment and are supported by cold-chain distribution. These can be great additions to your beer.

Making a fruit juice concentrate was, can you believe it, the final project of my Chemical Engineering degree. The process is complicated. It involves a huge amount of processing, which in the final product shows in a loss of flavour. Fruit juice made from concentrate is easy to transport, get hold of and straightforward to use. One can definitely see why they are so popular.

One of the most important things to note is that the fruit juice aroma is removed fairly early on in the process when making fruit juice from concentrate, in order to protect these volatile compounds. Aroma compounds are easily damaged and simply would not survive the evaporation process intact. They are later added back into the juice.

The difference in flavour between freshly squeezed orange juice and orange juice from concentrate is palpable, and that difference will probably be noticeable in your brew. The colour of a fruit juice concentrate, or the deterioration thereof, can be a good indicator of quality. Any overprocessing or storage in poor conditions will be evident in its colour.

I have worked with some excellent fresh juices and juice concentrates, and some terrible ones. I have learned over the years to make a judgement call based on the quality of the juice or concentrate I have in front of me. There is no better way, and there is no substitution for tasting the product. When making a beer – or any drink – from fruit, the quality of the raw material is always where I start.

There are many different options for the many types of fruits and juices that you can add to your home brew. Cherry is a common addition to *krieks*, passionfruit is added to sour beers, whilst red berries are often used in dark beers and citrus fruit such as grapefruit and oranges are used in IPA's.

WHEN SHOULD I ADD IT?
Kettle, fermenter, secondary fermentation.

ESSENCES

Fruit essence can come in a few different forms. The aroma that is removed during the fruit juice concentration process to protect it from the heat, can be separated and is sold on its own. It's usually clear and concentrated. It has uses in many other industries, including the perfume industry, and can even be an ingredient in sweets! It can also be used to enhance fruit beers.

However, I must admit that I am not a big fan of fruit essences. They can be narrow, one note and lack the complexity of fresh fruit. However, I get that, on a commercial scale, fruit essence can have its uses, especially when working with fruit with a muted nose. A good example would be blueberries or cherries – both fruits that don't have a strong or immediately recognisable smell. When a natural essence is combined with a pulp or purée, it can result in a beer that not only tastes great, but smells great too. My advice here: if you are going to use an essence, do so sparingly.

Artificial essences or flavourings tend to be made in a laboratory, often from raw materials that are not edible. Often the chemical compounds found in natural flavourings and artificial ones are actually the same, but overuse of these kinds of flavourings in beer is where I draw the line. For example, the difference between 'fake' cherry, such as cherry drops, and real, fresh cherries is vast and the fake version just isn't something I want to drink. I get that there are many beers out there with these kinds of tastes and flavours, and there are some that have become very popular, but it's just not what I want to produce.

WHEN SHOULD I ADD IT?
Prior to packaging.

DRIED FRUIT

Brewing with dried fruit can be delicious: think raisins, dried apricots and dried sloe berries. You will often get the most out of your dried fruit by rehydrating them before use – simply soaking them in water. A lot of dried fruit ends up sitting in a dusty cupboard weeks or months, so it's always worth washing thoroughly and sanitising with boiling water prior to use. Watch out for preservatives, additives or oils – you don't want those in your beer, so always check the ingredients list.

WHEN SHOULD I ADD IT?
Mash, kettle, fermenter, secondary fermentation.

TINCTURES

I think everyone should know how to make a tincture – not just for beer making, but for everyday life.

A tincture is the extract of a wanted substance (usually herbs or spices) using ethanol as the solvent. Throughout history, tinctures have been used for medicinal purposes, usually taken orally, with a few drops of the chosen tincture placed under the tongue for its full effect.

Using tinctures in beer making does have several advantages. Sometimes throwing your herbs, spices, flowers or fruit into your beer just isn't enough. Some flavours may not leech well at room temperature or extract well in beer at all. If you are using a mixture of different herbs and spices, you may get better flavour extraction from some over others.

Using a tincture can add an evenness to your flavour additions, so you add the exact pre-determined flavour to your beer, at the right intensity.

It also helps that by making a tincture in high-proof alcohol, this happens to sanitise your additional flavourings, considerably lowering the infection risk present when adding anything to fermenting or to a finished beer.

A tincture is more likely to leech flavour considerably faster than by adding it straight into the fermenter, so if you're looking for maximum flavour, quickly, tinctures are the way to go.

WHEN SHOULD I ADD IT?
Secondary fermentation, prior to packaging.

HOW TO MAKE A TINCTURE

1. Chop, grind or slice your flowers, herbs, spices, wood or fruit. The aim is to increase the surface area.
2. Place them in clean, dry mason jars.
3. Top up the jars with your alcohol. Vodka is generally preferred, due to its neutrality. Make sure there is approximately 2cm (¾in) of alcohol covering the surface.
4. Label and leave somewhere dark for 2–6 weeks. Dry ingredients may absorb the alcohol, so top up as needed.
5. Shake every three days.
6. Place your clean muslin cloth in your bowl and secure with bulldog clips. Strain your tincture.
7. With clean hands, gather the ends and squeeze. You want to squeeze out as much liquid as possible.
8. Filter the tincture again with a fine filter – a coffee filter would work well. If you don't have one, leave to settle overnight and use your muslin bag to filter again.
9. Fill your tincture bottles and label. Your tincture should last for several years.

YOU WILL NEED

2 MASON JARS WITH LIDS

BULLDOG CLIPS

FLOWERS, HERBS, SPICES, WOOD OR FRUIT

HIGH-PROOF ALCOHOL*

(Any grain-neutral spirit or vodka; 40 per cent ABV works well).

AMBER TINCTURE BOTTLES OR JARS

MUSLIN CLOTH OR COFFEE FILTERS (PREFERABLY BOTH)

*It is possible to make tinctures with solvents other than ethanol. If, for whatever reason, you don't want to use alcohol for your tincture, there are other options available to you, such as apple cider vinegar or glycerine. To be super clear, different solvents will have different levels of effectiveness. This is why alcohol has become the main solvent of choice for tinctures: it's almost uniformly effective.

5

WILD BREW STYLES

TOOLS OF THE TRADE

Brewing equipment is simpler than you think. The aim of this book was always to make brewing beer more accessible at home. People are often put off by the perceived complexity of homebrewing equipment, but in my experience, complicated equipment is just not necessary to make fantastic beer. It's perfectly possible to make delicious beer mainly with items you can already find in your kitchen. Just pay a visit to a homebrew shop or place an order online for the extra bits and pieces.

YOU WILL NEED

2 BIG POTS WITH LIDS

Each pot should be capable of holding approximately 35 litres of liquid. These will be used to mash, sparge and boil your brew.

2 MUSLIN CLOTHS OR NYLON BREW BAGS

Used for separating grain and hops from your brew.

COOLING RACK

You want a cooling rack that fits comfortably on top of your brewing pot.

SPOON

A long plastic spoon is perfect.

JUG

A large plastic jug that can hold at least 2 litres of liquid.

THERMOMETER

A digital or glass thermometer.

SEALED CONTAINER WITH LID (FERMENTER)

A 25-litre plastic container is perfect for the role of a fermenter. The standard homebrewing size is between 19 and 23 litres, so you will be able to follow recipes easily from a whole host of different sources. Make sure your plastic fermenting container is made from food-grade plastic and does not have any major scratches, as they can harbour bacteria. Plastic fermenters can be purchased from any homebrewing shop. Some recipes may require more than one fermenter.

HYDROMETER

The most important piece of equipment in a brewery, this tells you how alcoholic your beer is. You take the specific gravity of the beer at the start of fermentation (known as 'original gravity', or OG) and again at the end ('final gravity', or FG). The difference between these two numbers helps you calculate the ABV – you can use an online calculator to help you work this out.

BOTTLE CAPPER

Puts the caps on your bottles.

AIRLOCKS

These help to avoid oxidation of your beer by allowing CO_2 to escape, but not allowing air to enter your fermenter.

PLASTIC BUCKET

You can use this to store sanitising solution and all of your sanitised equipment.

PH PROBE OR PH STRIPS

Will help to keep your brew on track.

HIGH-LEVEL HOMEBREWING

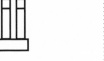

WOODEN BARREL OR OAK PIECES

If you want to take your brewing to the next level, I would highly recommend using 20-litre oak barrels. Be warned, these barrels are pricey, but treat them right and you should be able to get at least 10 uses out of them. You can also use oak pieces if you do not have a barrel.

BOTTLE BRUSH

For cleaning bottles, and also to get to all the nooks and crannies in the fermenter.

SIPHON TUBE

To help you move your beer from one container to the next.

TYPES OF BEER

Below are the wild brew styles that are included in the book,
with recipe examples on the following pages.

FARMHOUSE ALE

'Farmhouse ale' is an umbrella term for a wide range of beer styles that were produced in the working farms of what is now Belgium and northern France. As the name suggests, the farmhouse ale was the drink of the working farmer and was not generally brewed commercially. Farmers would brew in the winter when workload was light, and stockpile the beer for their thirsty seasonal workers in the coming summer months.

There was, once upon a time, a huge variety of different farmhouse ales. As you can imagine, each farmhouse would have used their own recipes, using a mixture of malted barley, unmalted barley, wheat or whatever grain they had to hand. Couple this with multiple different yeast strains and high fermentation temperatures, and farmhouse beers would have been massively varied, both in terms of flavour and quality.

The very seasonal nature of farmhouse work meant that many farmhouse brews had to be capable of long term storage. This gave way to two techniques to hold spoilage at bay. The first was to increase the hopping rate, the second was to increase the ABV. Both fairly handsome antibacterial techniques.

Two dominant beer styles emerged, anchored in these long-standing farmhouse brewing traditions. They were the *saison* and the *bière de garde*. Both of these styles are synonymous with the Farmhouse-style ale and, I would say, are the category's most famous members.

SAISON

Saison is the ultimate farmhouse beer. Famous for its funky flavours – think bubblegum, clove and banana – it's a style that developed in Wallonia, a French-speaking region of Belgium. Literally meaning 'season' in French, the *saison* is a close cousin of *bière de garde*, commonly found a few miles south in France. It typically has a lively carbonation, and is fruity on the nose with a fairly dry finish. Modern interpretations tend to be around 5–7 per cent ABV.

Over the years, many of these more rustic farmhouse brews, each as individual as the place that made them, were forgotten.

IPA

This is a pale ale that is made with extra hops, and is therefore often classified as a 'hoppy' beer. There are a huge variety of different styles of IPA beer, and they have become very popular in more recent times.

GOSE

The *gose* is a sour, salted wheat beer originating in the town of Goslar in northern central Germany. The *gose* as a beer style is a very old one, tracing its roots to over 1,000 years ago. The first mentions of gose appear in the Middle Ages, long before the usage of hops in beer was common. A mixture of herbs for bittering and flavouring, known as a *gruit*, would probably have been used instead. During this time period, the *gose* would probably have been fermented either spontaneously or with mixed wild cultures prevalent in the wood used to brew and ferment the beer. It is argued that the *gose*'s distinct saltiness comes from the highly saline River Gose, which runs through the town. When other nearby towns tried to recreate this popular beer's distinctive salty flavour, they did what any brewer now would do, and simply added a pinch of salt. The true reason for the *gose*'s salty nature has long been a source of contention, but one thing is for sure: this mineral quality is one of the beer style's most unique and recognisable features.

The *gose* style has evolved greatly since the Middle Ages, but a few stand-out attributes remain the same: its wheat beer base, its sourness and, of course, its salinity. The modern *gose* tends to be fairly muted in ABV, typically between 3 and 5 per cent. It's commonly spiced with coriander seed, has high carbonation levels and should be a thirst-quencher of a drink with a fairly dry finish. It must be noted that although this beer contains salt, it shouldn't taste salty: we are after a mineral quality here. I always say, if a *gose* tastes salty, then you've added too much salt!

BERLINER WEISSE

The Berliner Weisse has quite the historical claim to fame. It is said that during Napoleon Bonaparte's advance into Germany in the early 1800s, his troops affectionately named the style 'the Champagne of the North'.

The Berliner Weisse is a low-ABV, sour wheat beer made famous in Germany's capital, Berlin. Although the Berliner Weisse literally has the word 'Berlin' in its name, its origins are actually fairly cloudy. One of its most likely sources is the long-lost beer style, the Broyhan. The Broyhan was a beer with a very low ABV, typically less than 1.5 per cent. It was sometimes brewed with wheat, other times just barley – it was probably just brewed from whichever grains were available. This 'barely fermented' Broyhan brew first showed itself in Hanover in northern Germany during the sixteenth century. It proved to be popular and spread like wildfire across the north of the country, including its capital, Berlin. The theory goes that this popular Broyhan beer slowly merged into the Berliner Weisse. It's easy to see how: its ABV increasing slightly to around 3 per cent; its wheat beer base becoming a staple grain; and its tartness a stand-out feature of the style. And what happened to the original Broyhan? Like so many others, it was lost to the commercial lagers that came to dominate Germany.

The Berliner Weisse is ultimately a refreshing style, but for some, its tartness was a little too mouth-puckering. During the nineteenth century, it became fashionable to add flavoured syrups to help soften its acidity. These days in Berlin, you can find the Berliner Weisse served with a shot of raspberry syrup or herbaceous woodruff syrup. These syrups turn the beer bright pink or bright green respectively, and the concoction is typically served in a chalice and drunk through a straw.

The tourists lap it up! It really is an oddity of a beer. It is possible to find a Berliner Weisse without syrup in Berlin, but it does require a bit of hunting. It's well worth it, though.

In the UK, I've never seen a fruit syrup poured into a Berliner Weisse: it's just not done. The closest thing I can think of is a 'Snakebite & Black' (sometimes appropriately called a 'Nasty'), which consists of equal parts lager and cider and a shot of blackcurrant cordial – definitely not on the same page!

The truth is the Berliner Weisse is a beer style that lends itself beautifully to a fruit addition. It's quite common in the UK for fruit to be incorporated into the brew itself. I like to make mine with lime zest and juice for a zingy lime Berliner Weisse.

FLANDERS RED

The Flanders red is one of the most distinct beer styles in existence. Once you've tasted it, I promise you, you will never forget it. It's commonly compared to a Burgundy red wine, and while I do understand that comparison, I don't think it really does it justice. The Flanders red is an explosion of flavour. It has a rich, malty base and a plump fruitiness about it – mainly overripe cherries, plums and oranges. All of this flavour is beautifully balanced with a mouth-puckering vinegary lead sourness, and spicy vanilla undertones imparted by the oak barrels in which it is commonly aged.

The Flanders red originated in the West Flanders in Belgium. For centuries, the Belgians have made dark sour-based beer, most of which was, in all likelihood, spontaneously fermented. Beer was a product of its environment.

As brewing practices improved, brewers began to seek refinement from their beers. In England, they had a well-established system of blending different-aged beers together, especially the London porter. They would blend this highly sought-after and expensive old oak-aged beer with a young, spritely fresh beer. A young and enthusiastic Belgian called Eugene Rodenbach travelled to England to study beer making in preparation for taking over his family's Rodenbach brewery, which was based in West Flanders. At this time, Rodenbach brewery was being run by his mother, the very entrepreneurial Regina Wauters. The story goes that Eugene Rodenbach absorbed the English brewing techniques, namely maturing beer for long periods in oak and blending various batches together to create the perfect beer. Armed with this new knowledge and the unique terroir of West Flanders, in 1864 Eugene Rodenbach bought the brewery from his mother and the Rodenbach Flanders Red was born.

One of the things I love most about the Flanders red style is the beautiful dance between the many differing organisms that make up the beer. Yes, acetic acid (produced by *Acetobacter* bacteria) is the most dominant flavour, but it also contains *Saccharomyces* brewer's yeast, *Brettanomyces* yeast and lactic-acid producing organisms *Pediococcus* and *Lactobacillus* bacteria: it's a real melting pot of all the best of these differing organisms.

The world's best brewers of Flanders reds rely heavily on the blending of various batches to achieve the best of this style. While this requires a certain amount of commitment from a homebrewer, if you've come this far in this book, I do not for a second doubt your potential – avid homebrewers can be some of the most committed individuals. However, even if that is not possible, you can still use this recipe to make a delicious single batch of Flanders red.

OUD BRUIN

The Oud Bruin, also known as the Flanders brown, is an umbrella term for a host of both brown and red beers made famous in the East of Flanders, Belgium. Like its sister the Flanders red, the Oud Bruin style, literally meaning 'Old Brown', is known for taking advantage of the blending technique, blending together aged beer with younger versions.

Oud Bruins tend to be very malt forward, with lots of raisin and fig flavours. They are sour, but lack the vinegary sourness that dominates the Flanders red style. Generally, I would say they're on the lighter side of the perceived sour spectrum, although this is partly due to their malty backbone distracting the palate! Rather than being barrel-aged, Oud Bruins are usually matured in stainless-steel vats (you can use your plastic fermenter at home). Stainless steel is considerably easier to clean than oak barrels, which means the complex microorganisms are significantly more 'controllable'. This explains the lack of acetic characteristic in the Oud Bruin when compared with the Flanders red. It has a much less sharp acidic bite. It is essentially a subtly sour, sweet, malty brown ale.

LAMBIC

A product of spontaneous fermentation, lambic beers are the jewel in the crown of wild brews. Widely known as the 'Mother of All Beers', this Belgian beer style is a funky, sour, barnyard, horsey wheat beer. It's one of the few things all brewers will agree on: this is the pinnacle of brewing.

The lambic style is the oldest of all the existing beer styles, first appearing in written records in the fourteenth century.

Understandably, it is heavily steeped in Belgian tradition. While other beer trends have come and gone, the lambic has remained largely unchanged, incubated in the Senne river valley.

Lambics are fermented in large, shallow, swimming pool-type vats that are open to the air. These vats are known as 'coolships' and have long been used in the making of spontaneously fermented beer. The beginning of a lambic brew is fairly straightforward, with the exception of the use of old, skanky hops rather than the usually preferred fresh, green, spritely ones. The hot beer is placed into wide, shallow coolship vats, whose high surface area helps the beer to cool quickly. Wild yeasts and bacteria present in the air fall on to the cooling beer. In some cases, the steam rises up from the cooling beer, hits the exposed wooden rafters above, then condenses and slowly drips back into the coolship vats, bringing wild yeast and bacteria with it.

Lambics are one of the few beers on the market that are truly spontaneously fermented – although one might add that the areas of Pajottenland and Brussels, where lambics are made, have had centuries of conditioning. To say the region is well suited to the style is a bit of an understatement. The Senne river valley was once laden with fruit trees, a perfect place for wild yeasts and bacteria to thrive. The brewery buildings themselves also play an important role in the production of lambic beers, with thriving inner ecosystems. Their exposed wooden beams, their floors and their walls are all harbingers of the wild yeasts and bacteria that make the spontaneously fermented lambic beers what they are.

Because of the inherent yeast and bacterial spontaneity required when making a lambic beer, it is notoriously challenging to brew it at home. If you live in an area with lots of fruit trees, then for you things may be easier, but for me, in the middle of east London, this is certainly not the case. Be warned: the results can be highly variable. There are two methods of brewing a lambic I would advise you to try: one is the traditional open-top, spontaneously fermented lambic, which is very dependent on your environment; the other is inoculated fermentation.

OLD ALE

You might be surprised to see English old ale in this book, but it absolutely deserves to be here. Historically, English old ales were stored in oak barrels for long periods of time, and those barrels would almost certainly have contained wild yeast, which would have added to the complexity and richness of the old ale. It has been supposed that English ale-brewing practices inspired the Belgians to blend their brews, as it was common for taverns across the land to blend an expensive old ale with a younger one. But, whatever the real story, whether the English breweries inspired the Belgians or the Belgian breweries drove the English ones, we can be certain of one thing: both nations became brewing juggernauts, each with its own rich history. When it comes to who inspired who, it was probably a bit of both.

An old ale ranges from a dark amber to a rich dark brown. It's a fairly high-alcohol, malt-forward beer, filled with flavours of molasses and dried fruit, with nutty caramel notes in the mix, too. There is usually a sweet, almost vinous aroma about an old ale, akin to a port or a sherry. This beer should taste aged, with an almost dusty quality – in a good way, I promise! It's the kind of beer that brings up images of roaring fires and comfortable socks. This is as opulent as beer gets.

GUEUZE

A *gueuze* is a blend of one-year-old, two-year-old and three-year-old lambic beers. This blend of old and comparatively young beer is bottle conditioned. The young lambic tends to still contain some unfermentable sugars and viable yeast, and its sourness will probably be on the lighter side, whereas mature lambic beer should be flat, fiercely sour and full of character. The very best blenders manage to bring out the positive attributes of each beer. You are looking for a complex and beautiful balance.

To make a true *gueuze*, you have to have a fairly developed lambic homebrew set-up. It's good to get into the habit of making a batch of lambic on a yearly basis and hiding it away for storage. That way, when you're ready to make your *gueuze*, you've not only got several batches to choose from, but you can really focus on getting the packaging side of it right.

6

THE
RECIPES

THE BASIC METHOD

I have used the simplest of all grain-brewing methods, the 'brew in a bag' or BIAB technique. This method has minimal equipment costs and is very simple, highly adaptable and easy to clean up after. All winning factors, in my opinion! You can brew excellent beer using this technique, but I know that many of you will have your own brewing equipment set up already. Feel free to use the recipes in this chapter within your existing set-up. You may have to make a slight adjustment to account for the difference in brew efficiencies.

You'll need the equipment listed on page 100.

Mashing in

1. In a pot, heat your mash water to 75°C (167°F) (or slightly hotter if aiming for a higher mash temperature). Use your thermometer to check the temperature. Take off the heat once this temperature is reached.
2. Put your muslin cloth in the pot, securing the sides with clothes pegs or bulldog clips.
3. Gently stir all the malt into your water, keeping it within the constraints of the muslin cloth. Ensure all of the grains are fully wetted. The consistency should be like thick porridge.
4. Check the temperature. You want it to be 64–68°C (147–154°F). If it's too cold, turn the heat on. If it's too hot, leave the lid off to let it cool down.
5. Cover the pot with the lid and leave your mash for 1 hour. Insulate your pan if possible – the aim is to not let your mash drop below 63°C (145°F). I like to wrap a towel around my pot for insulation. Please make sure your heat is switched off if you do this – we don't want to start a fire!

Sparging

1. In your second pot, heat your sparge water (see page 24) to 79°C (174°F).
2. Remove the pegs securing the muslin cloth in your first pot and gather together the ends. Carefully lift the muslin bag containing the grains out of the first pot and place it in your second pot. Secure the sides of the cloth again with clothes pegs or bulldog clips. I find it's easier to do this at ground level. Be careful: the muslin bag is hot and heavy. You may need a friend to help you lift it.
3. The first pot will now contain the sweet, concentrated wort known as the first runnings. Do not allow to cool. Put this pot back on the stove and heat.
4. In the second pot, gently stir the mash for 10 minutes.
5. Once more, remove the pegs securing the muslin cloth and gather together the ends. Carefully lift the muslin bag containing the grains out of the pot. Place the cooling rack on the pot and rest the muslin bag on top, to allow any excess liquid to drip back into the pot. The spent grain can now be disposed of.
6. Using a jug, add the rinsed wort from the second pot into the first pot, then bring it to the boil.

Boil

1. At the start of the boil, add your boil hop, then 40 minutes later, add your 40-minute hop. Five minutes after that, add 1g kettle finings, if the recipe requires it. Leave the pan lid off throughout the boil.
2. After 1 hour from the start of the boil, add your 60-minute hop addition, if required, then turn off the heat. Leave to stand for 20 minutes.

Transfer

1. Sterilise your muslin cloth, fermenter and plastic jug.
2. Put your muslin cloth over the top of the fermenter and secure it with pegs. Using your plastic jug, pour the beer into your fermenter through the muslin sieve. This will remove any hops. Use a clean oven mitt or heat-protective glove here. Be careful, it is hot! (If you have any means of heat exchange to cool the beer quickly, use it now.)
3. Leave your beer to cool to 20°C (68°F). The quicker the beer cools, the better. Take an original gravity reading with your hydrometer, following the instructions written on the hydrometer's packaging.
4. Sprinkle your yeast onto the cooled beer in the fermenter, then place the fermenter somewhere warm (a room temperature of about 22°C/72°F would work) with the lid loosely placed upon it. If you have a bung and airlock, use them.

Fermentation

1. Three days after fermentation has begun, test the gravity of your beer again using the hydrometer. When the gravity reaches 1.012–1.016, add your fruit addition (if there is one).
2. Fermentation is complete once the gravity stops changing. This means that the yeast has probably consumed all the sugars it can. Your hydrometer should give the same reading for several days.
3. Move your fermenter to a cool space. A fridge would be superb, but a cellar or a cooler area of your home would also work. Your beer is now ready for packaging (see Chapter 6).

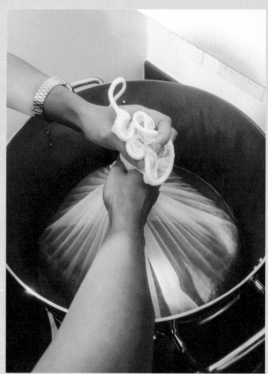

KVEIK NEW ENGLAND IPA

Kveik are traditional Norwegian farmhouse brewing yeasts. *Kveik* (pronounced 'kwike)', meaning 'yeast' in a Norwegian dialect, can in some ways make the ultimate homebrewed beers. They are particularly suited to the new homebrewer who has no way to control fermentation temperatures, because *kveik* yeasts are known for being able to ferment beer up to 40°C (104°F). The first time I heard this, I literally had to sit down!

Water	Hops	Yeast
Mash: 19 litres pre-boiled water	**Boil:** 2g Citra	Omega Yeast OYL091 Hornindal Kveik
Sparge: 11 litres pre-boiled water	**60 minutes:** 25g Cascade	
Malt	**Dry hop**	**Finings**
4.5kg crushed lager malt	**Final gravity:** 200g Citra (T90 Pellets) – cool to 20°C	No finings
1kg crushed wheat malt	**Final gravity:** 200g Simcoe (T90 Pellets) – cool to 20°C	
1.4kg crushed malted oats		
0.5kg flaked oats		

Mash temperature: 68°C (154°F)   **OG:** 1.064   **FG:** 1.012–1.014   **ABV:** 6.8–6.6 per cent

It's important to remember that kveik is not a beer style: you can brew almost anything with kveik yeast. I think it works perfectly with a New England-style IPA. The fruitiness of the yeast helps to add another layer of complication to this already beautiful beer style.

Typical warm-fermenting ale yeasts love to ferment at around 20°C (68°F), and when fermented at higher temperatures will kick out a huge amount of 'off' flavours that are boozy, plasticky and solvent-y. With kveik yeasts, we get none of that. They work well brewing higher-ABV beers and like to ferment at 25–40°C (77–104°F). They produce a lovely fruity, ester-filled, spicy profile and will also ferment extremely quickly. You can expect your primary fermentation to finish in as little as two days, and you may see activity only 30 minutes after pitching your yeast. Just as every farmhouse is different, there are different kveik yeasts available on the market. Look out for the different *kveik* strains – they will be named according to where they have been cultured.

Follow the **mashing in**, **sparging** and **boil** instructions from the **Basic Method** (page 112), then continue below.

Transfer

1. Sterilise your muslin cloth, fermenter and plastic jug.
2. Put your muslin cloth over the top of the fermenter and secure with pegs. Using your plastic jug, pour the beer into your fermenter through the muslin sieve. This

will remove any hops. Use a clean oven mitt or heat-protective glove. Be careful, it's hot! (If you have any means of heat exchange to cool the beer quickly, use it now.)

3. Leave your beer to cool to 32°C (90°F). The quicker the beer cools, the better. Take an original gravity reading with your hydrometer (make sure your test sample is at 20°C/68°F for accurate hydrometer reading).

4. Sprinkle or pour your yeast onto the cooled beer in the fermenter, then place the fermenter somewhere warm, with the lid loosely placed upon it. (If you have a bung and airlock, use them.)

Fermentation

1. Fermentation should become visibly active very quickly after pitching your *kveik* yeast.

2. Two days after fermentation has begun, test the gravity of your beer using your hydrometer. Fermentation is complete after the gravity stops changing. This means that the yeast has likely consumed all the sugars it can.

3. Move your fermenter to a cool space. You want to cool your beer down to 20°C (68°F) prior to dry hopping, and keep it at this cooler temperature if possible. You could put it in a fridge for a short time, or place it in a cellar or a cooler area of your home.

4. Remove the lid from your fermenter and sprinkle the T90 hop pellets into your beer.

5. Leave your beer for four days, then taste. If your beer is not hoppy enough, leave it for another day and taste again. You can leave your beer on the hops for a maximum of seven days. Do not be tempted to take the lid off and stir your beer – this will introduce oxygen into your beer, which will reduce its shelf life and produce 'off' flavours.

6. Chill your beer further by putting your fermenter in a colder space. A fridge would be ideal, but a cellar or a cooler area of your home would also work. The idea is to get your beer as cold as you can. Your beer is now ready for packaging (see Chapter 6).

RASPBERRY *SAISON*

Saison is the ultimate farmhouse beer. Famous for its funky flavours – think bubblegum, clove and banana – it's a style that developed in Wallonia, a French-speaking region of Belgium. Literally meaning 'season' in French, the *saison* is a close cousin of *bière de garde*, commonly found a few miles south in France. It typically has a lively carbonation and is fruity on the nose with a fairly dry finish. Modern interpretations tend to be around 5–7 per cent ABV.

I absolutely love the combination of raspberry with a *saison*. The fruity tang added by the raspberry works wonderfully with the *saison* style to make a drink that is complex as well as quaffable.

Water
Mash: 14 litres pre-boiled water
Sparge: 16 litres pre-boiled water

Malt
2.2kg crushed lager malt
2.2kg crushed Maris Otter malt,
    or any crushed pale malt
0.7kg malted oats

Hops
Boil: 2g Simcoe
40 minutes: 7g Simcoe
60 minutes: 15g Simcoe

Yeast
11g Belle *Saison* Lallemand yeast

Finings
Kettle finings (carrageenan)

Fruit
1kg raspberry purée

Mash temperature: 67°C (135°F)   **Original gravity (OG):** 1.052
Final gravity (FG): 1.008–1.006
ABV: 5.8–6% (your fruit addition should also increase the ABV slightly)

Follow the **Basic Method** on page 112.

THE KETTLE SOUR METHOD

There are many brewers out there who will tell you that kettle souring is cheating. Just so we are clear – yes, it is cheating. But it's also an important weapon in the brewer's arsenal – and what's a little cheating among friends? The method will produce a sour that is fairly one note when compared with a lambic or a Flanders red. This lack of complexity is usually the reason why some turn their noses up at this style, but I think that you don't always need complexity, but an easy-drinking, moreish beer you can enjoy in volume.

The kettle sour is normally fairly soft and fruity, and can have creamy overtones. It is known for being fast, souring in a matter of days rather than months or years. This speed is the reason the kettle sour is popular with brewers.

The method of brew itself is fairly typical until the beer is in the kettle and the boil takes place. There are a number of different ways of making a kettle sour, but my preferred method is outlined below.

Mashing in

1. In a pot, heat your mash water to 75°C (167°F) (or slightly hotter if aiming for a higher mash temperature). Use your thermometer to check the temperature. Turn off the heat once this temperature is reached.
2. Put your muslin cloth in the pot, securing the sides with clothes pegs or bulldog clips.
3. Gently stir all the malt into your water, keeping it within the constraints of the muslin cloth. Ensure all of the grains are fully wetted. The consistency should be like thick porridge.
4. Check the temperature. You want it to be 64–68°C (147–154°F). If it's too cold, turn the heat on. If it's too hot, leave the lid off to let it cool down.
5. Cover the pot with the lid and leave your mash for 60 minutes. Insulate your pan if possible. The aim is to not let the temperature of your mash drop below 63°C (145°F).

Sparging

1. In your second pot, heat your sparge water to 79°C (174°F).
2. Remove the pegs securing the muslin cloth in your first pot and gather together the ends. Carefully lift the muslin bag containing the grains out of the first pot and place it into your second pot. Secure the sides of the cloth again with clothes pegs or bulldog clips. I find it's easier to do this at ground level. Be careful: the muslin bag is hot and heavy. You may need a friend to help you lift it.
3. The first pot will now contain the sweet, concentrated wort known as the first runnings. Do not allow to cool. Put this pot back on the stove and heat.
4. In the second pot, gently stir the mash for 10 minutes.
5. Once more, remove the pegs securing the muslin cloth and gather together the ends. Carefully lift the muslin bag containing the grains out of the pot. Place the cooling rack on the pot and rest the muslin bag on top, to allow any excess liquid to drip back into the pot. The spent grain can now be disposed of.
6. Using a jug, add the rinsed wort from the second pot into the first pot, then bring it to the boil.

Inoculation

1. Boil the beer for 10 minutes, then turn off the heat.
2. Leave the beer to cool to 35°C (95°F), then add your live yogurt – 2 teaspoons of yogurt per litre of beer will suffice. This live yogurt contains *Lactobacillus* bacteria, which produces lactic acid.
3. Cover your container with the lid and create a tight seal. You can wrap the lid with cling film if necessary.
4. Leave overnight.
5. The next morning, check the pH of your beer. You want it to be less than 3.5pH. If not, leave for a further 4 hours and check again.
6. Once a pH of below 3.5 is reached, bring the beer to a boil. Boiling will kill the *Lactobacillus* bacteria.

Boil

1. Add your boil hop. Start the 60-minute boil countdown from now. 40 minutes in, add your 40-minute hop. Then, 5 minutes after the 40-minute hop addition, add 1g kettle finings, if the recipe requires it.
2. One hour after you added your boil hop, add your 60-minute hop addition and turn off the heat. Leave to stand for 20 minutes.

Transfer

1. Sterilise your muslin cloth, fermenter and plastic jug.
2. Put your muslin cloth over the top of the fermenter and secure with pegs. Using your plastic jug, pour the beer into your fermenter through the muslin sieve. This will remove any hops. (If you have any means of heat exchange, use it now.)
3. Leave your beer to cool to 20°C (68°F). The quicker the beer cools, the better. Take an original gravity reading with your hydrometer.

4. Sprinkle your yeast on to the cooled beer in the fermenter. Place the fermenter somewhere warm (a room temperature of about 22°C/72°F would work) with the lid loosely placed upon it. If you have a bung and airlock, use them.

Fermentation

1. Three days after fermentation has begun, test the gravity of your beer again using the hydrometer. When the gravity reaches 1.012 –1.016, add your fruit addition, if there is one.
2. Fermentation is complete after the gravity stops changing. This means that the yeast has probably consumed all the sugars it can. Your hydrometer should give the same reading for several days.
3. Test the pH of your beer. If you have added fruit into your sour beer, this will probably adjust the overall pH. In my experience, kettle sours shine at 3.1–3.2pH. I would advise you to taste your beer and ask yourself, 'Is it sour enough?' If not, you can add a small amount of lactic acid to slightly adjust the pH and bring it into this range.
4. Move your fermenter to a cool space. A fridge would be superb, but a cellar or a cooler area of your home would also work. Your beer is now ready for packaging (see Chapter 6).

Note

- Don't forget that hops are antibacterial and you are trying to create an environment where your *Lactobacillus* bacteria will thrive, so adding hops with active bacteria is counterproductive and a complete no-no. Make sure you make the bacteria inactive (i.e. kill it) by boiling the beer before you add the hops.

SOUR RASPBERRY *SAISON*

This combination of a sour beer on a *saison* base with the extra fruity punch from the raspberry just works. I've used the kettle souring method to achieve the 'sourness' in this recipe because it adds such a simple, clean sourness. With so much going on with this flavour profile – the floral, spicy and clove notes of the saison, plus the rich, full-flavoured raspberry – a clean sour adds a real drinkability to this beer.

Water
Mash: 14 litres pre-boiled water
Sparge: 16 litres pre-boiled water

Malt
2.2kg crushed lager malt
2.2kg crushed Maris Otter or any crushed pale malt
0.7kg malted oats

Hops
Boil: 2g Simcoe
40 minutes: 7g Simcoe
60 minutes: 15g Simcoe

Bacteria
250g live yogurt

Yeast
11g Belle *Saison* Lallemand yeast

Finings
Kettle finings (carrageenan)

Fruit
1kg raspberry purée

Additional
pH meter or pH strips
lactic acid (if needed)

Mash temperature: 67°C (153°F)   **OG:** 1.052   **FG:** 1.008–1.006
ABV: 5.8–6 per cent (your fruit addition should also increase the ABV slightly)

Follow the **Kettle Sour Method** on page 120.

GOSE

This is a sour, salted wheat beer. The distinct background saltiness of the beer is what marks this out from others, although be careful – while the beer contains salt it shouldn't actually taste salty, instead it should have more of a mineral flavour.

Water
Mash: 12 litres pre-boiled water
Sparge: 16 litres pre-boiled water

Malt
2.6kg crushed lager malt
2.1kg wheat malt

Hops
Boil: 6g Saaz
40 minutes: 15g Saaz
60 minutes: 30g Saaz

Bacteria
250g live yogurt

Yeast
11g Safale US05

Finings
Kettle finings (carrageenan)

Herbs and spices
55 minutes: 14g salt
55 minutes: 20g coriander seeds, crushed

Additional
pH meter or pH strips

Mash temperature: 67°C (153°F)   **OG:** 1.044   **FG:** 1.008   **ABV:** 4.7 per cent

Follow the **mashing in**, **sparging** and **inoculation** instructions in the **Kettle Sour Method** (page 120), then continue as below.

Continue following the **transfer** and **fermentation** instructions in the **Kettle Sour Method** (page 120).

Boil

1. Add your boil hop. Start the 60-minute boil countdown from now. At 40 minutes into your 60-minute boil, add your 40-minute hop. Then 5 minutes after the 40-minute hop addition, add 1g kettle finings (if the recipe requires it).
2. At around 55 minutes from the start of boil, add both the salt and the freshly crushed coriander seeds.
3. Five minutes later (60 minutes from the start of boil) add the 60-minute hop, then turn off the heat. Leave to stand for 20 minutes.

PASSION FRUIT *GOSE*

One of my most popular brews is Wild Card Brewery's Passion Fruit *Gose*. This beer started out as one I used to make at home. I fell in love with it, then decided to scale it up.

Water
Mash: 12 litres pre-boiled water
Sparge: 16 litres pre-boiled water

Malt
2.6kg crushed lager malt
2.1kg wheat malt

Hops
Boil: 6g Saaz
40 minutes: 15g Saaz
60 minutes: 30g Saaz

Bacteria
250g live yogurt

Yeast
11g Safale US05

Finings
Kettle finings (carrageenan)

Herbs and spices
55 minutes: 14g salt

Fruit
1kg passion fruit purée

Additional
pH meter or pH strips

Mash temperature: 67°C (153°F) **OG:** 1.044 **FG:** 1.008
ABV: 4.7 per cent (your fruit addition should also increase the ABV slightly)

This recipe is very similar to the regular gose recipe, with a few notable differences. I have added passion fruit purée and removed the coriander. The passion fruit is so overwhelmingly tropical that I find this recipe works better without the floral addition of the coriander.

Follow the **mashing in**, **sparging** and **inoculation** instructions in the **Kettle Sour Method** (page 120), then continue as below.

Boil

1. Add your boil hop. Start the 60-minute boil countdown from now. At 40 minutes into your 60-minute boil, add your 40-minute hop. Then 5 minutes after the 40-minute hop addition, add 1g kettle finings (if the recipe requires it).
2. At around 55 minutes from the start of boil, add the salt.
3. Five minutes later (60 minutes from the start of boil) add the 60-minute hop, then turn off the heat. Leave to stand for 20 minutes.

Continue following the **transfer** and **fermentation** instructions in the **Kettle Sour Method** (page 120).

THE PITCH AND WAIT SOUR METHOD

There are two main methods for brewing the delicious Berliner Weisse. One is the kettle sour method, as described on page 120, and the other is the 'pitch and wait' method, which I'm going to outline below. The kettle sour method includes a boil after the addition of the *Lactobacillus* bacteria, so the bacteria is killed and the risk of infection is low. The pitch and wait method is trickier. The *Lactobacillus* bacteria is pitched at the end of the brew, prior to the addition of brewer's yeast. The *Lactobacillus* bacteria is never killed off with this method, so it's very important that every item you use is thoroughly sterilised. In fact, I would recommend separating all equipment that comes into contact with the bacteria and using it for only sour brewing in the future. This method is what you would call the 'traditional method', but be warned: it is more difficult and it will take longer to brew. Traditionally, a Berliner Weisse is made with a decoction mash, which is a method in which the temperature of the mash is changed in steps. This is very equipment dependent. If you have a Braumeister brewing kit, then by all means try it. I am, however, an English brewer, and single-infusion mashes are what we do! Most malts are well modified enough to make step mashes unnecessary, although I am certain my German counterparts would disagree with me!

Mashing in

1. In a pot, heat your mash water to 75°C (167°F) (or slightly hotter if aiming for a higher mash temperature). Use your thermometer to check the temperature. Turn off the heat once this temperature is reached.
2. Put your muslin cloth in the pot, securing the sides with clothes pegs or bulldog clips.
3. Gently stir all the malt into your water, keeping it within the constraints of the muslin cloth. Ensure all of the grains are fully wetted. The consistency should be like thick porridge.
4. Check the temperature. You want it to be 64–68°C (147–154°F). If it's too cold, turn the heat on; if it's too hot, leave the lid off to let it cool down.
5. Cover with the pot lid and leave your mash for 60 minutes. Insulate your pan if possible. The aim is to not let the temperature of your mash drop below 63°C (145°F).

Sparging

1. In your second pot, heat your sparge water to 79°C (174°F).
2. Remove the pegs securing the muslin cloth in your first pot and gather together the ends. Carefully lift the muslin bag containing the grains out of the first pot and place it in your second pot. Secure the sides of the cloth again with clothes pegs or bulldog clips. I find it's easier to do this at ground level. Be careful: the muslin bag is hot and heavy. You may need a friend to help you lift it.
3. The first pot will now contain the sweet, concentrated wort known as the first runnings. Do not allow to cool. Put this pot back on the stove and heat.
4. In the second pot, gently stir the mash for 10 minutes.
5. Once more, remove the pegs securing the

muslin cloth and gather together the ends. Carefully lift the muslin bag containing the grains out of the pot. Place the cooling rack on the pot and rest the muslin bag on top, to allow any excess liquid to drip back into the pot. The spent grain can now be disposed of.

6. Using a jug, add the rinsed wort from the second pot into the first pot, then bring it to the boil.

Boil

1. At the start of the boil, add your boil hop. It is important only a minimal amount of hops are added, as hops are antimicrobial and will inhibit the growth of *Lactobacillus* bacteria later. Around 15 minutes before the end of the boil, add 1g kettle finings. Leave the pan lid off throughout the boil.

2. Then, 60 minutes after the start of the boil, turn off the heat. Leave to stand for 20 minutes.

Transfer

1. Sterilise your muslin cloth, fermenter and plastic jug.

2. Put your muslin cloth over the top of the fermenter and secure it with pegs. Using your plastic jug, pour the beer into your fermenter through the muslin bag sieve. This will remove any hops. Use a clean oven mitt or heat-protective glove here. Be careful, it is hot! (If you have any means of heat exchange to cool the beer quickly, use it now.)

3. Leave your beer to cool to 35°C (95°F). The quicker the beer cools, the better. Take an original gravity reading with your hydrometer.

Inoculation

1. Sprinkle your chosen bacteria on to the cooled beer in the fermenter, then place

the fermenter somewhere warm.

2. Cover your container with the lid and create a tight seal. You can wrap the lid with cling film if necessary.

3. Leave overnight.

4. Check the pH of your beer. You want it to be 3.5–3.6pH. If not, leave for a further 2 hours and check again.

5. Your beer should have now cooled to room temperature (about 22°C/72°F). Add your brewer's yeast.

Fermentation

1. Three days after fermentation has begun, test the gravity of your beer again using the hydrometer. When the gravity reaches 1.012–1.016, add your fruit addition (if there is one).

2. Fermentation is complete after the gravity stops changing. This means that the yeast has probably consumed all the sugars it can. Your hydrometer should give the same reading for several days. After terminal gravity has been reached, leave it for a further day.

3. Test the pH of your beer. If you have added fruit to your sour beer, this will probably adjust the overall pH. Taste your beer to see if it is sour enough. If not, you can add a small amount of lactic acid to slightly adjust the pH and bring it into this range.

4. Put your fermenter in a cool space. A fridge would be superb, but a cellar or a cooler area of your home would also work. Your beer is now ready for packaging (see Chapter 6).

BERLINER WEISSE

Water
Mash: 10 litres water
Sparge: 19 litres water

Malt
2.3kg crushed lager malt
1.4kg wheat malt

Hops
Boil: 9g Hallertau Mittelfrüh

Bacteria
Wild Brew Sour Pitch

Yeast
11g Safale US05

Finings
Kettle finings (carrageenan)

Fruit
1.012 gravity or 5 minutes before end of boil: zest of 10 limes
1.012 gravity: juice of 10 limes

Additional
pH meter or pH strips

Mash temperature: 66°C (151°F)   **OG:** 1.033   **FG:** 1.008   **ABV:** 3.3%   **IBU:** 4

PITCH AND WAIT METHOD

Follow the **Pitch and Wait Sour** method (page 128), then continue below.

INOCULATED AND MIXED FERMENTATION METHOD

Follow the **mashing in**, **sparging**, **boil** and **transfer** instructions in the **Basic Method** (page 112), then continue below.

Fermentation

1. Five days after fermentation has begun, test the gravity of your beer using a hydrometer. Fermentation is complete after the gravity stops changing. This means that the yeast has probably consumed all the sugars it can.

2. After terminal gravity has been reached, you will need to transfer the beer into a secondary fermenter, either your oak barrel (see page 86 for how to fill a barrel) or another fermentation container. To do this, place the primary fermenter (the one that currently contains the beer) at waist height – on a kitchen counter, for example – and place the secondary fermenter lower down. Use a siphon tube to transfer the beer from one container to the other, leaving behind the compact yeast in the bottom of the fermenter.

3. If you are inoculating further, add your culture to the secondary fermenter.

4. Keep the secondary fermenter somewhere warm. Leave it for 6 months (up to 24 months).

5. After 6 months of ageing, if you do not have an oak barrel, add your wine-soaked oak to the secondary fermenter if desired. Leave for a week, then taste the beer. If the oak flavour is not intense enough, leave for another day, then taste again. Repeat until you are happy with the oak balance of the beer. See page 86 for more tips on working with oak pieces.

6. Move your fermenter into a cool space. A fridge would be superb, but a cellar or a cooler area of your home would also work. Your beer is now ready for packaging.

FLANDERS RED

Water

Mash: 16 litres pre-boiled water

Sparge: 14 litres pre-boiled water

Malt

1.5kg crushed lager malt

0.7kg wheat malt

3kg crushed Vienna malt

0.85kg light crystal malt

0.45kg dark crystal malt

Hops

Boil: 15g Hallertauer Mittelfrüher

40 minutes: 10g Hallertauer Mittelfrüher

60 minutes: 20g Hallertauer Mittelfrüher

Bacteria

Wyeast 3763 Roeselare Belgian Sour Blend

Yeast

11g Safale US05

Finings

Kettle finings (carrageenan)

Additional

pH meter or pH strips

siphon tube

oak barrel, or French oak cubes (medium toast).

Mash temperature: 66°C (151°F)   **OG:** 1.055   **FG:** 1.008   **ABV:** 6.2%   **IBU:** 8

Follow the **mashing in**, **sparging**, **boil** and **transfer** instructions in the **Basic Method** (page 112), then continue below.

Fermentation

1. Five days after fermentation has begun, test the gravity of your beer using a hydrometer. Fermentation is complete after the gravity stops changing. This means that the yeast has probably consumed all the sugars it can.
2. After terminal gravity has been reached, you will need to transfer the beer into a secondary fermenter, either your oak barrel (see page 86 for how to fill a barrel) or another fermentation container. To do this, place the primary fermenter (the one that currently contains the beer) at waist height – on a kitchen counter, for example – and place the secondary fermenter lower down. Use a siphon tube to transfer the beer from one container to the other, leaving behind the compact yeast in the bottom of the fermenter.
3. If you are inoculating further, add your culture to the secondary fermenter.
4. Keep the secondary fermenter somewhere warm. Leave it for 6 months (up to 24 months).
5. After 6 months of ageing, if you do not have an oak barrel, add your wine-soaked oak to the secondary fermenter if desired. Leave for a week, then taste the beer. If the oak flavour is not intense enough, leave for another day, then taste again. Repeat until you are happy with the oak balance of the beer. See page 86 for more tips.
6. Move your fermenter into a cool space. A fridge would be superb, but a cellar or a cooler area of your home would also work. Your beer is now ready for packaging.

Note

- If you don't feel it has enough of that acetic acid flavour, blend in a small quantity of malt vinegar prior to packaging.
- Adding a tiny amount of unpasteurised vinegar in with your other bacteria will also produce a strong acetic flavour.

OUD BRUIN

Water
Mash: 19 litres water
Sparge: 12 litres water

Malt
4.7kg crushed lager malt
1.15kg caramunich crushed malt
1kg crushed Vienna malt
0.36kg crushed Special B malt

Hops
Boil: 50g Hallertauer
Mittelfrüher
40 minutes: 20g Hallertauer
Mittelfrüher
60 minutes: 20g Hallertauer
Mittelfrüher

Bacteria
Wyeast 3763 Roeselare Belgian
Sour Blend

Yeast
11g Safale US05

Finings
Kettle finings (carrageenan)

Additional
pH meter or pH strips
second fermenter

Mash temperature: 65°C (149°F)   **OG:** 1.066   **FG:** 1.012   **ABV:** 7.1%   **IBU:** 24

Follow the **mashing in**, **sparging**, **boil** and **transfer** instructions in the **Basic Method** (page 112), then continue below.

Fermentation

1. Five days after fermentation has begun, test the gravity of your beer using a hydrometer. Fermentation is complete after the gravity stops changing. This means that the yeast has probably consumed all the sugars it can.

2. After terminal gravity has been reached, you will need to transfer the beer into a secondary fermenter, either your oak barrel (see page 86 for how to fill a barrel) or another fermentation container. To do this, place the primary fermenter (the one that currently contains the beer) at waist height – on a kitchen counter, for example – and place the secondary fermenter lower down. Use a siphon tube to transfer the beer from one container to the other, leaving behind the compact yeast in the bottom of the fermenter.

3. If you are inoculating further, add your culture to the secondary fermenter.

4. Keep the secondary fermenter somewhere warm. Leave it for 6 months (up to 24 months).

5. After 6 months of ageing, if you do not have an oak barrel, add your wine-soaked oak to the secondary fermenter if desired. Leave for a week, then taste the beer. If the oak flavour is not intense enough, leave for another day, then taste again. Repeat until you are happy with the oak balance of the beer. See page 86 for more tips on working with oak pieces.

6. Move your fermenter into a cool space. A fridge would be superb, but a cellar or a cooler area of your home would also work. Your beer is now ready for packaging.

Note

- Oud Bruins are typically not barrel-aged. You can use a fermenter as a secondary fermentation vessel.

LAMBIC

Water
Mash: 16 litres water
Sparge: 13 litres water

Malt
3.5kg crushed lager malt
2.2kg wheat malt

Hops
Boil: 18g Saaz
or
Boil: 115g any old cheesy low-
  alpha acid hop, such as
  3-year-old Saaz

Bacteria
Wyeast 3278 Belgian Lambic
  Blend

Yeast
11g Safale US05

Finings
Kettle finings (carrageenan)

Additional
oak barrel (or oak pieces)
glass carboy and bung (or plastic
  fermenter with lid and airlock)

Mash temperature: 65°C (149°F) **OG:** 1.052 **FG:** 1.010 (Variable) **ABV:** 5.5% **IBU:** 8

INOCULATED AND MIXED FERMENTATION METHOD
Follow the **mashing in**, **sparging**, **boil** and **transfer** instructions in the **Basic Method** (page 112), then continue below.

Fermentation
1. Five days after fermentation has begun, test the gravity of your beer using a hydrometer. Fermentation is complete after the gravity stops changing. This means that the yeast has probably consumed all the sugars it can.
2. After terminal gravity has been reached, you will need to transfer the beer into a secondary fermenter, either your oak barrel (see page 86 for how to fill a barrel) or another fermentation container. To do this, place the primary fermenter (the one that currently contains the beer) at waist height – on a kitchen counter, for example – and place the secondary fermenter lower down. Use a siphon tube to transfer the beer from one container to the other, leaving behind the compact yeast in the bottom of the fermenter.
3. If you are inoculating further, add your culture to the secondary fermenter.
4. Keep the secondary fermenter somewhere warm. Leave it for 6 months (up to 24 months).
5. After 6 months of ageing, if you do not have an oak barrel, add your wine-soaked oak to the secondary fermenter if desired. Leave for a week, then taste the beer. If the oak flavour is not intense enough, leave for another day, then taste again. Repeat until you are happy with the oak balance of the beer. See page 86 for more tips on working with oak pieces.
6. Move your fermenter into a cool space. A fridge would be superb, but a cellar or a cooler area of your home would also work. Your beer is now ready for packaging.

Transfer
1. Sanitise your muslin cloth, pot and plastic jug.
2. Put your muslin cloth over the top of the pot and secure with pegs. Using your plastic jug, pour the beer into your pot through the muslin sieve. This will remove any hops.

Inoculation

1. Move your full pot into the environment you want to use to inoculate your beer. You'll probably need help to carry the hot liquid. Be careful!
2. Take the lid off your pot and leave for 24 hours. Depending on your environment, you may want to put a clean muslin cloth over the top of the pot to prevent large bits from falling into it.

SPONTANEOUS FERMENTATION METHOD

Follow the **mashing in**, **sparging** and **boil** instructions in the **Basic Method** (page 112), then continue as below.

Transfer

1. Place your cooled beer at waist height, for example on a kitchen counter (you may need some help lifting it) and place your fermenter at a lower height. Use a siphon tube to transfer beer from the pot to the fermenter. A glass carboy with a bung and airlock can be very useful as a fermenter here, as it will allow you to see the activity of the various microorganisms, but you can also choose to ferment directly into a barrel, or you can use a regular plastic fermenter with an airlock. Fill the fermenter as full as you can, this will reduce the beer-to-air interface.

Fermentation

1. Keep your fermenter somewhere where it won't be disturbed, at a temperature of 17–23°C (63–73°F).
2. You should begin to see signs of activity in the first 2 weeks. Leave it for 6 months.
3. After 9–12 months of ageing, if you are happy with the flavour of your lambic (and if you don't have an oak barrel), add your oak pieces if desired. Leave for a week, then taste the beer. If the oak flavour is not intense enough, leave for another day, then taste again. Repeat until you are happy with the oak balance of the beer.
4. Your beer is ready for packaging when the gravity stops changing. As we are working with some very slow organisms, make sure the hydrometer gives the same reading for about 6 weeks.
5. Move your fermenter to a cool space. A fridge would be superb, but a cellar or a cooler area of your home would also work. Your beer is now ready for packaging (see Chapter 6).

Notes on lambic

- Do not drink the beer in the first 2 months of fermentation: food-poisoning organisms will probably be present during this time.
- Regularly top up the water in your airlock to prevent it drying out.
- A white, cream or grey pellicle appearing at the beer-to-air interface is fine. Do not disturb it or pop it. (A pellicle is a thin biofilm looks like a bit like an unpopped bubble.) Pellicles with a strong colour – black, green or red, for example – are a bad sign. If this happens, dump the beer.
- If your beer develops long, slimy, stringy tendrils, don't worry. (see the *Pediococcus* section on page 66). Leave your beer for longer, and this should clear up.
- Before tasting your beer, ensure it has a pH of less than 4.5 and that it has an ABV of at least 3 per cent. Be careful not to oxygenate your beer when sampling.
- Life-cycle dominance in your beer should be:
  Enterobacter – 7 days
  Saccharomyces – 2 weeks
  Pediococcus – 4 months
  Brettanomyces – 8 months
  Oxidative yeasts – 8 months*
- For the very best results, leave the beer to age for 1–3 years prior to packaging.

* From Wyeast Laboratories, (wyeastlab.com/brewing-brettanomyces-yeast-cultures-and-lactic-acid-bacteria)

GUEUZE

To make a true *gueuze*, you have to have a fairly developed lambic homebrew set-up. I recommend you make a batch of lambic on a yearly basis and hide it away for storage.

Beer

3 batches of lambic beer (see recipe on page 136): 1 year old, 2 years old and 3 years old

Equipment

measuring cylinder
sterilised fermenter
several cups
pen and paper

1. Taste all three batches of beer and try to pick out the characteristics you like in each. For example, you might note that lambic no. 1 is the most tart and sour, and lambic no. 2 has some very nice barnyard/horsey flavours, while lambic no. 3 is very dry, with some nice pineapple notes. Write these down. With so many beers to try, it can become confusing, fast.
2. Using several cups, mix together different blends of the three batches to find your preferred combination. Don't forget to measure the amount you have added of each one every time.
3. Once you've found your preferred blend, scale up the quantities and blend together the quantities you've calculated in a clean fermenter.
4. Your beer is now ready for packaging (see Chapter 6).
5. Any leftover lambic that hasn't been used in your blend can be poured into a fermenter with some fruit. This would make a delicious framboise (with raspberries) or *kriek* (with cherries).

OLD ALE

Old ale ranges from a dark amber to a rich dark brown. It's a fairly high-alcohol, malt-forward beer, filled with flavours of molasses and dried fruit, with nutty caramel notes in the mix as well.

Water
Mash: 20 litres pre-boiled water
Sparge: 10 litres pre-boiled water

Malt
5.9kg crushed pale malt
0.7kg wheat malt
0.3kg crushed chocolate malt
1kg light crystal malt
0.45kg crushed brown malt

Hops
Boil: 38g Challanger
40 minutes: 40g East Kent Goldings
60 minutes: 40g East Kent Goldings

Yeast
11g Safale US05

Finings
Kettle finings (carrageenan)

Additional
oak barrel, or French oak cubes (medium toast)

Mash temperature: 67°C (153°F)   **OG:** 1.068   **FG:** 1.015   **ABV:** 7%   **IBU:** 40

Follow the **mashing in**, **sparging**, **boil** and **transfer** instructions in the **Basic Method** (page 112), then continue below.

Fermentation

1. Five days after fermentation has begun, test the gravity of your beer using a hydrometer. Fermentation is complete after the gravity stops changing. This means that the yeast has probably consumed all the sugars it can.

2. After terminal gravity has been reached, you will need to transfer the beer into a secondary fermenter, either your oak barrel (see page 86 for how to fill a barrel) or another fermentation container. To do this, place the primary fermenter (the one that currently contains the beer) at waist height – on a kitchen counter, for example – and place the secondary fermenter lower down. Use a siphon tube to transfer the beer from one container to the other, leaving behind the compact yeast in the bottom of the fermenter.

3. If you are inoculating further, add your culture to the secondary fermenter.

4. Keep the secondary fermenter somewhere warm. Leave it for 6 months (up to 24 months).

5. After 6 months of ageing, if you do not have an oak barrel, add your wine-soaked oak to the secondary fermenter if desired. Leave for a week, then taste the beer. If the oak flavour is not intense enough, leave for another day, then taste again. Repeat until you are happy with the oak balance of the beer. See page 86 for more tips on working with oak pieces.

6. Move your fermenter into a cool space. A fridge would be superb, but a cellar or a cooler area of your home would also work. Your beer is now ready for packaging.

7

PACKAGING
YOUR BEER

PACKAGING

Now that you've made your delicious beer, it's time to package it! Packaging is one of those jobs that just doesn't get the attention it should. If beer brewing was a touring band, the lead singer would be the brewing process, the lead guitarist would be dry hopping, the cool bass player would be barrel ageing, and yeast would play the drums. Packaging, meanwhile, wouldn't even get to be in the band: it would be the roadie carrying all the gear, wistfully looking at the rest of the band on stage, night after night, stealing all that spotlight. But without the roadie, the gigs wouldn't happen – and the same goes for packaging. It's a vital part of the process.

Good packaging can take a great beer to supersonic levels, while poor packaging can easily make a great beer taste average. Before we get down to the bottling, there are two key areas within packaging that make all the difference: one is your carbonation level, and the other is hygiene.

Over the following pages, I will break down the key elements to both, along with essential equipment. These will ensure both a successful and optimal wild brew at home.

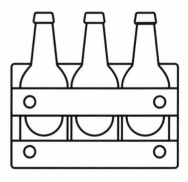

HYGIENE

Let's get the boring stuff out of the way first. They say that the life of a
professional brewer is 80 per cent cleaning and 20 per cent paperwork.
That's pretty accurate. Let's just say, you soon get used to cleaning literally
any item quickly, without fuss and with total accuracy.

There are three levels of cleanliness I employ in my professional and homebrewing life. Professionally, I just have better equipment and bigger tanks to deal with, but the principles and need for cleanliness are essentially the same.

The three levels are:

PHYSICALLY CLEAN

All physical matter removed, and the item cleaned with physical abrasion and water. The standard here is 'Would I eat off it?'.

CHEMICALLY CLEAN

Cleaned with Oxiclean or sodium percarbonate. (Washing-up liquid can be used, but only if the item is thoroughly rinsed afterwards.)

MICROBIOLOGICALLY CLEAN

Sanitised with a product like Star San. Note: sanitising and sterilising are not the same thing. Sanitisers reduce the levels of microbiological contaminants responsible for spoilage to negligible levels. Sterilisers remove all microbiological life.

Different pieces of equipment in a brewery require different standards of cleanliness. A fermenter should always be sanitised, taken up to the microbiologically clean level, but for the mash tun, being physically clean is enough – it should be taken up to the chemically clean level every couple of brews.

These standards apply when working with stainless steel, which is non-tainting, non-fouling and very easy to clean. Simply working with stainless steel eliminates a lot of potential hygiene issues.

However, in most homebrew set-ups (including my own), plastic is employed. Approach plastic, especially plastic fermenters, with caution. Plastic taints and, most importantly, it scratches. These scratches can potentially harbour bacteria and wild yeasts. I would advise getting all homebrew plastic equipment up to microbiologically clean standards before use. You should also replace your fermenters every so often if they begin to take on colour, if they have a lingering smell or if they are heavily scratched.

CLEANING BREWING EQUIPMENT

1. Fill your bucket with warm water and give your smaller items a thorough clean with cleaning solution and the soft side of a kitchen sponge. Larger items, like the big pots and your fermenter, can be cleaned in the kitchen sink – or in the bath, if you have sympathetic housemates.
2. Thoroughly rinse all items to remove all traces of cleaning solution.
3. Make up a sanitising solution in your bucket according to the packet instructions. Add your muslin cloth or nylon brew bag, spoon, jug, thermometer and hydrometer, and leave them until ready to use. (Note: if you are using Star San, it is known as a 'last line' sanitiser, which means you don't have to rinse it with water.)
4. Add some sanitising solution to your fermenter, then cover with lids until ready to use.

YOU WILL NEED

PLASTIC BUCKET

SANITIZING SOLUTION

KITCHEN SPONGE

CLEANING SOLUTION
Oxiclean or sodium percarbonate.

CLEANING BOTTLES

You can buy either buy brand new bottles or reuse and recycle old ones. Adopt the same approach as you would for a fermenter. A bottle has to be physically clean, chemically clean and microbiologically clean. You can buy glass bottles in a variety of sizes: 330ml (11.5oz), 500ml (17oz) or 750ml (25oz) are the most commonly available in the UK, while 355ml (12oz) and 650ml (22oz) are popular sizes in the US. When I make beers like lambics or a gueuze, I bottle them in 750ml (25oz) champagne bottles. There's something about a champagne bottle that screams 'fancy'. (It's likely the champagne part!)

CLEANING USED BOTTLES
1. Empty the dregs of beer from your bottles into the sink. Rinse your bottles immediately after use, as this will make your job easier in the long run. Cleaning dried-on yeast trub is no fun!
2. Rinse out the bottles with water.

3. To remove the bottle labels, soak your bottles in hot water for an hour, then peel off.

4. Fill a bucket with cleaning solution and hot water.

5. Use your bottle brush to clean each bottle, getting into all of the nooks and crannies. Then rinse.

6. Pour away the soapy water, then rinse the bucket, making sure it is very clean. Make up a sterilising solution according to the packet instructions.

7. Dip each bottle into the sterilising solution, making sure the inside of each is thoroughly coated.

8. Leave your bottles to dry, neck down, on your drying rack or bottle tree. (Make sure the rack is also clean and sanitised before you begin.)

CLEANING NEW BOTTLES

1. Rinse out the bottles with water.

2. Make up a sanitising solution in your bucket according to the packet instructions.

3. Dip each bottle into the sterilising solution, making sure the inside is thoroughly coated.

4. Leave your bottles to dry, neck down, on your drying rack or bottle tree.

YOU WILL NEED

PLASTIC BUCKET

SANITIZING SOLUTION

CLEANING SOLUTION

Oxiclean or sodium percarbonate – washing-up liquid can be used, but only if the bottle is thoroughly rinsed out afterwards.

BOTTLE BRUSH

BOTTLE TREE OR DRYING RACK

CLEANING OAK BARRELS

One of the easiest ways to avoid barrel drama is to immediately fill your barrel with your next beer after emptying it of its previous contents. If you can, you want to refill your barrel on the same day – or, at the latest, the next day. You should include a hot-water rinse of your barrel in between filling, where possible. This is to remove the build-up of trub (dead yeast) that is likely to be pooled at the bottom of the barrel, but can also cover the rough surfaces anywhere on the inside of the barrel. Over time, this trub build-up will lead to yeast autolysis (see page 179) and you will begin to get 'off' flavours from your barrel-aged beer. Don't worry too much about the hot water killing your yeasts or bacteria: they should be burrowed deeply enough into the wood for this not to be a significant issue. If you get into the habit of completing a hot water rinse this after every barrel emptying, it will help to keep your barrel in tip-top condition. It is also possible to chase one beer with another – in other words, rather than removing all of the previous beer, simply topping it up. Honestly, it depends how much you liked the previous set of organisms souring or maturing your beer.

1. Within 24 hours of emptying your oak barrel of beer, you should have your next beer ready to put into the barrel. If you have exceeded this 24-hour period, see 'Rehydrating' on page 157.

2. Rinse out your barrel with hot water (approx. 45–50°C/113–122°F should be adequate). If you are using a small barrel, you should be able to do this by hand, by adding hot water to it, then placing a wooden shive (the plug used to reseal a barrel) in the hole and physically shaking the container. Empty and repeat three times. If you are using a large, full-size barrel, you can use a barrel rinser (if you have one). Most brewers do if they clean casks regularly. A barrel rinser consists of a small rack on which to rest the barrel, with a spray ball on its head that allows water to fully reach the insides of the barrel. If you don't have a barrel rinser, you can still rinse large barrels by hand. Again, fill the barrel with water, place a wooden shive in the hole and physically roll the barrel around. Empty and repeat three times.

3. Repeat until the water leaving the barrel runs clear. Your barrel is ready for re-filling.

YOU WILL NEED

HOT WATER

WOODEN SHIVE

CLEANING OAK PIECES

It's good practice to sanitise any item you are going to add to your beer, even your oak pieces, cubes, staves, spirals, etc. A good way to sanitise oak pieces is by boiling them. This also has the desirable effect of toning down the harsh intensity of your oak, especially if it's fresh and hasn't been in contact with any alcohol previously.

1. Place your water in a saucepan or pot on the stove and bring to the boil.
2. Add your oak pieces and boil for 5 minutes.
3. Drain. Your oak pieces are now ready to use.
4. If you are going to soak your oak pieces in wine or a spirit, now is the time to do it. Do not re-boil your oak after soaking, as it will remove some of your hard-earned flavour.

YOU WILL NEED

WATER

LARGE SAUCEPAN OR POT

PROBLEM BARRELS

It's rare for brewers to get hold of freshly made oak barrels, and it's much more likely a barrel will be on its second, third or even fourth use by the time it's in your hands. Brewers tend to like the additional flavours that previous uses can add, whether it's been used to store wine, whisky, rum, hot sauce or soy sauce, to name but a few. It also helps that these previously used barrels are considerably cheaper than brand new ones! Brewers as a whole are some of the cheapest people I've ever met (and yes, I do include myself in this assessment!). So, if you can get a hold of a good barrel on the cheap, the tips below should help you to assess the barrel and hopefully solve any problems.

I should also add that, while I assume you will make every effort to refill your barrel on the same day, I am also not foolish enough to assume that every brewer set-up is organised enough to be able to achieve this. I know how it is: people get busy, things fall by the wayside, and consequently barrels don't get refilled. So, I'm going to give you some tips on what to do in such a situation. I'm going to assume you've treated a barrel in the worst way it is possible for a brewer to treat a barrel, and I'm going to show you how we are going to pull it back from the brink. I should warn you: it's not possible to save every barrel, but if you are faced with a leaky, smelly one, you should take the steps outlined below.

Assess the situation
If your barrel has been sitting empty for a little while – either in transport, at the brewery, in your homebrew club or in your house – the first thing I would suggest you do is assess the situation.

Open the bung and sniff the barrel. It should smell of wood and its previous contents – so if it was a wine barrel, it should smell of wood and wine. The same goes for whisky. You definitely shouldn't smell mould or any other 'off' flavour. If the barrel smells 'clean', then that's a great place to start. If it doesn't, that's officially a bad place to start. You will have no choice but to thoroughly clean your barrel, which usually includes much more than a hot water rinse (see 'Mouldy barrels', opposite).

Next, you should have a look inside your barrel. I use a dentist's mirror and a torch to have a really good look around my barrels. You're looking for any obvious wood defects. Any staves that are out of place may require a whack with a mallet to put back where they should be. If you see gaps between the staves, that implies you'll have to do some barrel rehydration (see opposite). Cracks in the wood near the bunghole can be an issue: they may not necessarily leak, but they may let in too much oxygen. Check how far the crack goes – is it on the surface, or does it go through the whole stave? While you're having a look, check the toasting on the inside of your barrel. It should be an even brown coating and fairly smooth – a lighter brown for a lighter toast and a darker brown for a heavier toast. If your barrel is charred, this should show itself by an almost black interior. A charred barrel may look damaged, but the thing you need to look out for here are blisters on the wood: they can harbour bacteria. This process of carefully inspecting your barrels is also helpful as it's not always possible to receive a full history of where your barrel has been when you first obtain it.

Tartrate crystals and blisters

Ex-wine barrels in particular can have a build-up of a substance known as tartrate crystals. They sparkle when light is shone on them, and if there is a build-up in your wine barrel, they should be removed, as, like blisters, they can harbour bacteria. The way to remove both blisters and tartrate crystals is to take off the head of the barrel and physically remove them using a wallpaper scraper. Pressure washing would also work. At this point, though, I would question the viability of doing this. Rather than going to all this effort listed above, it may be easier (and cheaper) to buy another used barrel in better condition.

Rehydrating

Let's assume your barrel smells 'clean' – so it smells of wood, plus its previous contents. The next thing you should look at is the barrel's physicality. Have any of the metal hoops around the barrel slipped or moved downwards? Barrels develop something I can describe as a tan line where the metal hoops are meant to be. It's immediately obvious if they have slipped out of place or are loose, and this is a sign that the barrel has shrunk in size and has therefore become dehydrated. It's easy to remedy, but if you miss this sign and add your beer to a dehydrated barrel, it may end up all over the floor, leaking through gaps.
Follow these simple steps:

- Fill your barrel with hot water. Assuming it is leaky, make sure you do this outside, or somewhere with adequate drainage.

- Move your hoops into place – follow those tan lines!

- Wet the outside of the barrel.

- Leave the barrel for 24 hours.

- Empty the barrel of water the next day and sniff it to check for mould (see below).

- Assuming it smells fine, refill the barrel with hot water. Repeat this process until the barrel no longer leaks.

Mouldy barrels

If your barrel smells of mould or doesn't smell 'clean', you have a few further options. If you have a steam cleaner, use that – steam is one of the most effective cleaning tools when it comes to working with wood. If not, then an alkaline chemical clean using a sodium percarbonate solution should work. You can use a citric acid solution to neutralise. Just follow the steps below:

- Fill the barrel with water to two-thirds full.

- Add your sodium percarbonate at a dosing rate of 1g per litre for mild spoilage and 3g per litre for more serious spoilage.

- Top up your barrel with water and leave the solution to work for 24 hours.

- Drain the barrel and refill with water until two-thirds full.

- Add your citric acid at a dosing rate of 1g per litre.

- Top up your barrel with water and leave overnight.

- Drain the barrel, then rinse it thoroughly with water and leave it to dry.

- Once it's dry, smell the barrel again. It should now smell 'clean'. If not, repeat the cleaning process above. If it still smells of mould after that, throw the barrel away.

CARBONATION

After all that cleaning, you must be exhausted!
But now it's on to the fun part: carbonation.

So, your beer is brewed, fermented, aged and ready to package. The one thing that's missing? BUBBLES! Yes, you need to add carbon dioxide to your beer. There are a few different ways you can do this, depending on your set-up at home.

Carbon dioxide has the power to lift a beer, to propel its aroma and to cleanse your palate. When CO_2 is dissolved in beer, it actually lowers its pH slightly, making your beer more acidic. This has the effect of pulling all of your lovely flavours into razor-sharp focus. An under-carbonated beer can taste flabby, wide and unfocused. Under-carbonation can, at best, be a distraction. At worst, it can ruin a beer.

The first thing you have to decide is how much CO_2 you want in your beer. This is quite a difficult question for a first timer to answer. CO_2 is measured in volumes so, to give you some context: your average cask beer will be

TYPICAL CARBONATION LEVEL OF BEER ACCORDING TO BEER STYLE

BEER STYLE	ADVISED CARBONATION LEVELS VOLUME CO_2
IPS	2.2–2.5
Lager	2.3–2.7
Saison	2.3–2.8
Berliner Weisse	2.4–3.5
Gose	2.4–3.5
Oud Bruin	2.2–2.6
Flanders red	2.2–2.6
Lambic	2.7–4.5
Framboise	2.7–4.5
Kriek	2.7–4.5
Gueze	2.7–4.5
Old ale	1.8–2.5

0.87 volumes CO_2, while a can of cola or fizzy pop is usually around 3.1 volumes CO_2, and a bottle of Champagne tends to sit at around a whopping 6 volumes CO_2. That's why Champagne bottles have special corks – to allow for the considerably higher levels of carbonation. The average Champagne bottle holds 6.2 bar of pressure! Luckily enough, there is handy guidance available that helps brewers decide what their carbonation levels should be – see opposite and below. Personal choice is, of course, a factor: I like to carbonate my beers to 2.2–2.5 volumes CO_2.

Make sure you take the carbonation levels of your beers into consideration when you are

choosing the type of bottle you want to package into. Highly carbonated beers require a bottle and closure that can withstand their carbonation. For example, it's a safe bet to use Champagne bottles and Champagne corks for highly carbonated lambics.

Residual carbonation

Without you doing anything, your beer will already be holding some level of carbonation. Depending on the temperature of your beer and the container it has been stored in, we can estimate the existing carbonation levels.

The amount of CO_2 a beer will absorb is dependent on its temperature. Take the highest temperature a beer has achieved while in storage after the gravity has become constant as the temperature for your residual CO_2 calculations.

If you have stored your beer in a barrel, you can divide the calculated residual carbonation by 2 to achieve an approximate CO_2 level. This is due to the porosity of a barrel.

RESIDUAL CARBONATION CHART

TEMPERATURES	VOLUMES CO_2
8.3°C (47°F)	1.21
10°C (50°F)	1.15
11.7°C (53°F)	1.09
13.3°C (56°F)	1.04
15°C (59°F)	0.988
16.7°C (62°F)	0.940
18.3°C (65°F)	0.894
20°C (68°F)	0.850
21.7°C (71°F)	0.807
23.3°C (74°F)	0.767
25°C (77°F)	0.728
26.7°C (80°F)	0.691
28.3°C (83°F)	0.655

From Brew Your Own (byo.com/resource/carbonation-priming-chart/)

Add nothing method

It's perfectly possible to go from secondary fermenter straight to bottling without adding anything. There will probably be enough yeast for some activity, but your carbonation levels will be very low. In a bottle, this would work better with very complex sour beers. CO2 physically lifts a beer's aroma up to your nose, so naturally it does enhance the perception of flavour. You would need a strong-flavoured beer to overcome this lack of aroma propulsion. This style of beer would also suit being served relatively flat because of its sourness. The sharp focus I mentioned earlier (as a result of the small drop in pH undergone by most beers after carbonation) is unnecessary here due to the beer style's natural propensity towards a low pH.

Add-sugar method

This is the simplest method of getting CO^2 into your beer, and I'm sure it's probably what most of you who are reading this will do.

You simply mix a little bit of sugar into your beer prior to bottling. The residual yeast will consume the sugar and produce CO^2 as a consequence. You have just have to put your bottled beer somewhere fairly warm for a few weeks, then it should be ready to serve – fizz and all. See opposite.

There are lots of different types of sugar on the market. For the purposes of carbonation, I advise you to always keep it simple. One of

PRIMING RATES FOR SUCROSE

SUCROSE	VOLUMES CO₂ PER 19 LITRES
28.3g (1oz)	0.37
42.5g (1½oz)	0.56
56.7g (2oz)	0.75
70.9g (2½oz)	0.93
85g (3oz)	1.12
99.2g (3½oz)	1.31
113g (4oz)	1.49
128g (4½oz)	1.68
142g (5oz)	1.87
156g (5½oz)	2.05
170g (6oz)	2.24
184g (6½oz)	2.43
198g (7oz)	2.61
213g (7½oz)	2.8
227g (8oz)	2.99
241g (8½oz)	3.17
255 (9oz)	3.36

From Brew Your Own (byo.com/resource/carbonation-priming-chart/)

PRIMING RATES FOR GLUCOSE

GLUCOSE	VOLUMES CO₂ PER 19 LITRES
28.3g (1oz)	0.34
42.5g (1½oz)	0.51
56.7g (2oz)	0.68
70.9g (2½oz)	0.85
85g (3oz)	1.02
99.2g (3½oz)	1.19
113g (4oz)	1.36
128g (4½oz)	1.53
142g (5oz)	1.70
156g (5½oz)	1.87
170g (6oz)	2.04
184g (6½oz)	2.21
198g (7oz)	2.37
213g (7½oz)	2.54
227g (8oz)	2.71
241g (8½oz)	2.88
255 (9oz)	3.05

From Brew Your Own (byo.com/resource/carbonation-priming-chart/)

Above: Bottling beer using a bottle capper.

the biggest issues with the sugar method is its inconsistency. If you don't mix your sugar into your beer correctly, you may end up with one bottle with too much sugar, which explodes, and another bottle with not enough sugar, which will end up being flat and disappointing. The last thing you want to do is add complex sugars into the mix – it's hard enough to get it right with the simple ones. So I would say a big fat no to honey, maple syrup or golden syrup – they are far too complex and contain too many long-chain sugars. I would also be against adding fruit purely as a sugar source for the purposes of carbonation. Yes, most fruits do contain mostly simple sugars, but each fruit is different, and unless you've got a detailed

spec sheet showing which sugars your fruit contains, don't go there. It is hard to get the amount of fruit required for good carbonation correct. If you want to include fruit for flavour, adding it at primary or secondary fermentation is the safer way to avoid exploding bottles. As a side note, the threshold for the amount of fruit you would have to add to get correctly carbonated beer is probably much lower than the amount that would give you a deliciously fruity beer.

Ordinary table sugar, sucrose, that you buy from the shop, is fine for use as a priming sugar. Glucose is also a good priming sugar.

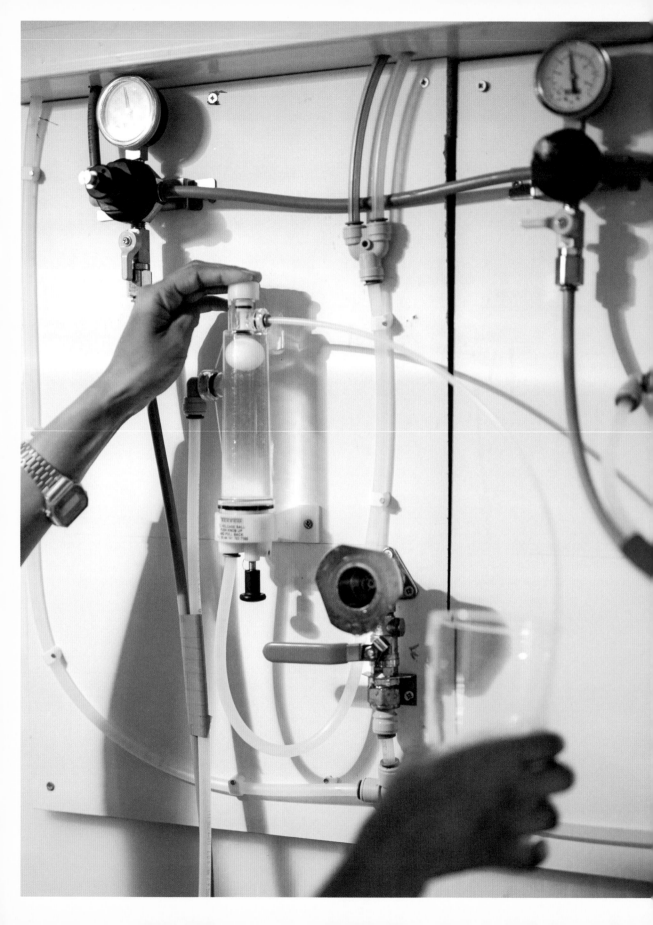

In order to calculate the total target carbonation of your beer, you need to add together the existing residual carbonation of your beer with the carbonation level that the priming sugar will add.

In other words:

**Target carbonation =
residual carbonation + priming carbonation**

You can also use online calculators to get your priming dosing right. Northern Brewer (www.northernbrewer.com) and More Beer (www.morebeer.com) both have very good priming calculators.

Re-yeasting

Because of the type of beers we are making, some special considerations do have to be made. Beers containing *Brettanomyces* yeasts, for example, or sugar-consuming bacteria will complicate things somewhat. We have a situation where multiple microorganisms will want to consume the sugar as a food source, and each organism will produce its own by-products, which can have a positive – or negative – impact on the overall flavour of the beer.

If you choose to add sugar to your barrel-aged beer, but don't add a new yeast source, chances are *Brettanomyces* will be the dominant yeast type. Bear in mind that *Brettanomyces* yeasts are slow fermenters, so you will have to lay your bottles down for a considerable amount of time in order to achieve your desired carbonation levels. After it's taken so long to make a gueuze, you may choose not to wait the extra number of months it's going to take for *Brettanomyces* yeasts to do their business.

You can add a fresh *Saccharomyces cerevisiae* yeast source into your beer with your priming sugar in order to speed things up. For a normal homebrew size (around 20 litres of beer), I would advise adding approximately 1.5–2g of yeast, which works out at about 0.5 billion cells per litre. You will need to rehydrate your yeast in warm water, at a temperature of approximately 30–35°C (86–95°F). You can choose from a whole host of yeasts at this stage, but I would recommend something neutral if you're really happy with the flavour of your beer. Yeasts like Safale US05 or Danstar's Nottingham work well as priming yeasts. You may also want to add a Champagne yeast for some of your more highly acidic beers.

It is also possible to re-pitch your beer with *Brettanomyces* yeast prior to bottling. Again, this method will take time, but it is a good way to add extra funky flavour to your beer.

Forced carbonation

Forced carbonation is the adding of CO_2 directly into your beer with a canister of CO_2 gas. It has quite a few positives over the sugar method in that it's more consistent, but on the downside, it requires a lot more equipment – dedicated equipment. The thought of putting these kinds of wild beers anywhere near my carbonation stone makes me shudder. The chance of infecting the brewery with wild microorganisms is not one that I want to take.

Some of you may already be set up to force carbonate, and if you are, it is a perfectly fine way to carbonate these kinds of beers.

SECONDARY FERMENTATION IN BARREL OR FERMENTER

1. Make sure all of your equipment has been cleaned and sanitised (see pages 147–53). Check your barrel is clean and ready for use (see pages 152–7).

2. Place your container of fermented beer at waist height – on a kitchen counter, for example – and place the barrel lower down. Use the siphon tube to start siphoning your fermented beer into your oak barrel or your second fermenter.

3. If you want to add any fruit in secondary fermentation, or you want to add some wood cubes (if not using a barrel) or some extra microbes, now is a good time. Pour your extra ingredient into your fermenter or barrel while it is siphoning. This will aid the even mixing with your beer. Adding fruit directly into your oak barrel is possible, but it is difficult to clean out afterwards.

4. Make sure you stop just before you reach the trub or the layer of yeast at the bottom of your fermenter.

5. Seal your barrel or second fermenter and leave it to age.

YOU WILL NEED

THE BEER YOU HAVE FERMENTED

SIPHON TUBE

FERMENTER OR OAK BARREL

BOTTLING YOUR BEER

1. Make sure all of your bottles have been cleaned and prepared (see pages 148–9).
2. Dissolve your sugar in a small amount of boiling water. Make sure the sugar is completely dissolved. Leave it to cool.
3. If you are re-yeasting your beer, rehydrate the yeast now.
4. Place your container of fermented beer at waist height – on a kitchen counter, for example – and position the bottling bucket lower down. Use the siphon tube to start siphoning your fermented beer into your bottling bucket.
5. While it is siphoning, pour the cooled sugar water and rehydrated yeast slurry into the bottling bucket. This will aid the even mixing of the sugar with your beer.
6. Make sure you stop just before you reach the trub or the layer of yeast at the bottom of the fermenter.
7. Take your bottling bucket and place it at a comfortable height (you don't want to be crouching uncomfortably for the next hour!).
8. Attach your sanitised bottling wand to the tap at the bottom of your bottling bucket.
9. Put your bottle wand into the first bottle. There is a push valve at the bottom of the wand that allows beer to flow when pressure is applied. The valve closes when you release the pressure (when the bottle is filled and you move the bottle away from the wand).
10. Use the bottle capper to cap the bottle.
11. Repeat steps 8–10 until your whole bottling bucket is empty.

YOU WILL NEED

BOTTLES

SUGAR

YEAST (OPTIONAL)

FERMENTER
Filled with the beer you want to bottle.

SIPHON TUBE

BOTTLING BUCKET (WITH A TAP)

BOTTLING WAND

BOTTLE CAPPER

8

WHEN THINGS
GO WRONG

OFF FLAVOURS

When brewing any beer, things can go wrong at times.
Be prepared for that. The true skill is knowing when to
package, when to blend and when to say 'There's nothing
more I can do here,' and move on.

I would advise any brewer to taste their beer. Then taste it again. Then taste it some more. Your taste buds are the most important part of the process, and no matter what recipe you're making, the key question absolutely has to be: 'Does this actually taste good?'

When brewing, I will taste the raw water, the malt, the spent grain, first runnings (at the start of the sparge), last runnings (at the end of the sparge) and the beer going into the fermenter. Then I'll taste it several times throughout the fermentation and packaging process. Doing it all the time builds up your taste memory: anything that doesn't taste as it should will quickly become apparent when you mentally compare notes between that and a previous brew.

Becoming a beer sommelier made me a better brewer, but long before I went legit, I started taking up every opportunity possible to improve my palate.

So if you can, get together with some friends, buy an off-flavour kit and get training. An off-flavour kit typically has concentrated vials of particular 'off' flavours, which you can use to spike a neutral beer. For your neutral beer, it's important to choose something fairly bland, especially for novices. Isolating specific aromas can be quite tricky if you're doing it for the first time, so it makes sense to make it easy for yourself. In the interests of not getting sued, I am not going to name names here, but there is a specific lager used in

flavour training all over the UK, because it has the dubious honour of being named The Blandest Beer of Them All. Take from that what you will.

There are many more 'off' flavours than those listed here, but these are the ones that come up time and time again. They are largely avoidable, and, with a little knowledge, you can even pull your beer back from the brink of some of them. As I have said before, though, part of making great beer is knowing when to cut your losses and dump the lot.

ACETIC

Smells like: Vinegar, sour.

Causes: Bacterial spoilage in beer.

The science: *Acetobacter* bacteria is generally airborne. It causes the oxidation of ethanol into acetic acid. Acetic acid in solution is more commonly known as vinegar. This process requires oxygen – *Acetobacter* bacteria cannot grow without it.

Commonly found in: Spoiled cask beer or an unclean bar.

How to fix: The presence of acetic acid can be entirely appropriate in certain sours, for example a Flanders red (page 106) or a light use in lambics (page 108). If your cask beer has turned sour, though, you have no choice but to dump it. To avoid this happening again in the future, have good sanitisation procedures and avoid the oxygen exposure of your beer.

ACETALDEHYDE

Smells like: Green apple.

Causes: There are two main causes. The first can be classified as general fermentation issues – including poor yeast health, rapid fermentations, high fermentation temperatures, low yeast pitching rates, poor wort aeration, and pitching finings too soon, causing the yeast to flocculate (i.e. drop out of the beer). The second cause, which is less common, is the exposure of your beer to oxygen.

The science:
- Acetaldehyde is an intermediate compound produced when yeast converts glucose into ethanol. It is present in all primary fermentations. If your fermentation is healthy, then most of the acetaldehyde will be converted into ethanol. In problematic fermentations, the acetaldehyde conversion to ethanol remains incomplete, and the compound becomes detectable.
- The second cause of acetaldehyde is the oxidation of ethanol back into acetaldehyde. Oxidation usually produces other recognisable 'off' flavours as well.
- Bacterial contaminants, like *Acetobacter* and *Zymomonas*, can also cause acetaldehyde. If this is the case, I would expect to see other telltale signs, like the beer souring.

Commonly found in: Young beer or old cask beer.

How to fix: Keep beer on the yeast for a few days after final gravity has been reached. Healthy yeast should 'mop up' acetaldehyde and clean up your beer. Krausening should also help (see Diacetyl on page 174).

BUTYRIC ACID

Smells like: Baby sick, bile, rancid cheese.

Causes: Infection; poor hygiene; bacterial spoilage in wort production or during fermentation; use of spoiled sugar syrups.

The science: Bacteria from the *Clostridium* genus produce this 'off' flavour. The bacteria are generally spore-forming and anaerobic, which means no oxygen is required – in fact, CO_2 has been shown to be a stimulatory environment for the bacteria's growth. As a side note, butyric acid is present in the human gut, and is responsible for the smell of vomit.

Commonly found in: Any beer where sugar syrup has been used; kettle sours.

How to fix: To avoid it happening again in future, have good hygiene procedures, especially during wort production. Some species of *Brettanomyces* convert butyric acid into ethyl butyrate at low levels. This has much more pleasant aromas of ripe pineapple and tropical fruits. So, try adding some Brett – I would say pineapple is far preferable to vomit any day of the week!

CHLOROPHENOL

Smells like: Medicinal, antiseptic, plastic.

Causes: Too much chlorine in your feed water; chlorinated cleaners not rinsed off properly; bacterial contamination after the boil; poor-quality old water hoses; wild yeast infection.

The science: Chlorine and/or chloramine is regularly added to our tap water in order to disinfect it. This prevents us from getting sick from a variety of bacteria, viruses and parasitic protozoa that could otherwise thrive in our tap water. Phenols found in beer react with these compounds, producing chlorophenols. Chlorophenols can generally be detected by the human tongue at very low thresholds.

Commonly found in: Any beer.

How to fix: In my experience, medicinal flavours do not improve over time. You'd be better off dumping the beer and starting again. Prevention is key with chlorophenol-based 'off' flavours.
- If your water source is the cause, try boiling it prior to use to remove chlorine. Boil for 15 minutes, then allow it to cool. Campden tablets added to your brewing water can reduce your chloramine levels.
- Closely follow manufacturer's instructions when using chlorinated-based cleaners and sanitisers, or avoid their use altogether.
- Good hygiene procedures can help, especially when it comes to your fermenter. Look out for any nicks or scratches in your fermenter: these are potential hiding places for a variety of microorganisms.

DIACETYL OR VDK

Smells like: Butterscotch, popcorn. Can also give a creamy mouthfeel.

Causes: Poor yeast management; chilling beer before fermentation is fully complete and not allowing yeast to go through its mopping-up phase; bacterial infection (common in dirty bar lines).

The science: Yeast produces diacetyl as part of normal fermentation. One of the intermediate compounds produced in the production of an amino acid called valine is acetolactate. Acetolactate can be converted to diacetyl in an oxidation reaction. Towards the end of fermentation, the yeast will consume, or 'mop up' this diacetyl, reducing its presence in your beer. If you remove your beer from the yeast too soon, this can interrupt the 'mopping up' of this diacetyl. Diacetyl can also be produced as part of bacterial contamination. Lactic acid-producing bacteria *Pediococcus* also produces diacetyl, as do some species of *Lactobacillus*.

Commonly found in: Lagers, any beer and dirty bar lines. Can be a deliberate part of the flavour profile of brown English ales.

How to fix:

- First, try a diacetyl rest. Let the beer sit at 18°C+ (64°F+) for 2–3 days at the end of fermentation, prior to chilling the beer and moving it off the yeast. Some diacetyl rests do take longer – I have had lagers take seven days before the diacetyl is acceptably reduced.

- Add a fresh source of yeast to your beer. One of the best techniques for doing this is to 'krausen' your beer. Brew and ferment a second batch of beer. The yeast will usually be at what we call 'high krausen' about two days into your fermentation. You can recognise this stage visually: the foam on top of your beer will be thick, almost meringue-like, and your fermentation will be at its most active during this time. Add some of this actively fermenting beer into your problem diacetyl beer. The fresh yeast should clean up your beer considerably after a few days.

- In my experience, some yeasts are more prone to noticeable diacetyl production than others, so think carefully about your yeast selection in the future.

- Make sure your brewing environment is kept clean. Ensure bottles are fully sanitised to prevent bacterial infection when packaging.

- If diacetyl is significantly present in beer that has already been bottled, I would dump the beer.

DIMETHYL SULPHIDE (DMS)

Smells like: Creamed sweetcorn.

Causes: Problems at the end of the boil, i.e. not having a vigorous or long-enough boil; the storage of hot wort; fermentation issues; using lightly kilned malt; bacterial infection.

The science: The precursor to DMS is a compound called S-methyl methionine (SMM). This compound is produced during the germination of barley (the preserve of maltsters). SMM is typically driven away during the process of kilning the barley. The lightest Pilsner or lager malts are very lightly kilned, which means their SMM levels can remain higher than those pale malts that are kilned for longer. When heated during the mash or boil, SMM is reduced into DMS, which in turn is driven off during the boiling process.

Commonly found in: Lagers.

How to fix: To prevent DMS in your beer, ensure that you have a vigorous rolling boil for an hour. DMS is driven off during the boil, so make sure that you don't cover your beer during this period, and do not allow condensate to fall back into your beer.
- Make sure you cool your beer quickly at the end of the boil – wherever possible, don't allow your beer to gently cool.
- CO_2 produced during fermentation drives off DMS, so healthy fermentations are a must.
- DMS in lagers is common – sometimes by design – and is not always unpleasant. If it's just a touch of DMS, that's OK.
- If caused by bacterial infection, this 'off' flavour tends to present as rancid, cooked vegetables. Throw the beer away and improve your hygiene.

ETHYL ACETATE

Smells like: Nail varnish remover, solvent.

Causes: Too high a fermentation temperature; stressed yeast; underpitched yeast; wild yeast infection.

The science: In small quantities, ethyl acetate can have a pleasant pear-like aroma, but too much and a distinctly unpleasant nail-varnish-remover smell becomes apparent. Ethyl acetate is a common ester produced during fermentation. At higher temperatures, more ethyl acetate tends to be produced. Different yeast strains will produce different levels of ethyl acetate.

Commonly found in: Any beer, but especially high-ABV beers and barrel-aged beers.

How to fix: These solvent flavours don't tend to improve over time, so I'd advise you to throw away the beer. To prevent this from happening in future, stop your beer from fermenting at too warm a temperature – try moving it to a cooler part of your living space. Different yeast strains will produce different levels of ethyl acetate, so choose your yeast wisely. Make sure you are increasing the amount of yeast you are pitching if you are making a higher ABV beer.

LIGHTSTRUCK

Smells like: Skunk, marijuana.

Causes: UV light.

The science: Beer is light-sensitive. The famous skunky flavour of lightstruck beer, 3-methyl-2-butene-1-thiol, is derived from isohumulones present in hops when beer is in contact with sunlight. This flavour is present in many commercial beers packaged in clear bottles! Lime wedge, anyone?

Commonly found in: Beer stored in clear, green or blue bottles, or secondary fermented in clear containers.

How to fix: Once developed, it is difficult to shift. Generally, be suspicious of beer in clear bottles. You can prevent lightstruck by keeping your beer in the dark and bottling in brown bottles. If you have clear glass carboys for the maturation of your beer, block out the light as much as possible by wrapping it in cloth or a bin bag. I have an old polo neck I dress my glass carboy in.

METALLIC

Smells like: Coins, rust, ink.

Causes: Contact with poor-quality metal; lipid oxidation.

The science: Metallic flavours most commonly come from metal that has leached into your beer from contact with said metal. Metallic contamination in your water source is also possible, old water pipes or well water, for example.

Commonly found in: Any beer that has been in contact with leached metal; beers with added fats.

How to fix: The root cause has to be found in order to prevent this happening again in the future. Check over your brewing equipment for rusty spots or exposed metal. Use stainless steel, glass or food-grade plastic in your brewing set-up. Metallic flavours don't tend to fade – in fact, they often become more pronounced over time.

OXIDATION

Smells like: Wet cardboard, paper, honey, sherry.

Causes: Beer ageing; exposure to oxygen; poor packaging and beer storage conditions.

The science: One of the major compounds recognised in the oxidation of beer is trans-2-nonenal. It's particularly present in beer that has been stored at too-warm a temperature.

Commonly found in: Aged beer.

How to fix: After oxygenation of your wort at the beginning of fermentation to aid the yeast, you should then avoid oxygen wherever possible. The most common time to pick up oxygen is when you are transferring from one fermenter to another, or when you are packaging. Avoid splashing your beer around and purge with CO_2 (replace air with CO_2) where possible. Cooler beer-storage temperatures tend to slow the oxidation process. Old or aged beer will pick up these 'off' flavours over time, so, especially in the case of hoppy beers, drink fresh!

PHENOLIC

Smells like: Cloves, spice, barnyard.

Causes: Formed from yeast during fermentation; a sign of wild yeast infection.

The science:
* The phenol 4-Vinyl guaiacol (4VG) is largely responsible for these spicy flavours, which are caused by the decarboxylation of ferulic acid. In wheat beers and in many Belgian *saisons*, these flavours – in the right quantities – are highly desirable. Yeasts are specially selected for their signature clove-like flavours in the production of Bavarian *hefeweizens*. High fermentation temperatures promote the increased production of 4VG.
* *Brettanomyces* yeasts can produce more barnyard flavours; another phenol, named 4-ethyl phenol, can largely take responsibility for that.

Commonly found in: Wheat beers, saisons, barrel-aged beers.

How to fix: The root cause has to be found in order to prevent this happening again in the future. Check over your brewing equipment for rusty spots or exposed metal. Use stainless steel, glass or food-grade plastic in your brewing set-up. Metallic flavours don't tend to fade – in fact, they often become more pronounced over time.

SULPHUR

Smells like: Struck matches, eggs, rotten eggs.

Causes: Beer youth; poor yeast health; high gypsum levels in water treatment; yeast autolysis; bacterial contamination.

The science: Hydrogen sulphide H^2S, which smells eggy, is produced by yeast as part of normal fermentation. It tends to be scrubbed from the beer during primary fermentation and beer conditioning. It can also be caused by bacterial contamination. Sulphur dioxide SO^2, however, smells more like a struck match. Some yeasts are more prone than others to produce sulphur dioxide flavours.

Commonly found in: Young beer, lager.

How to fix:
- Give your beer more time.
- Sulphur can be quite volatile, which means it dissipates quickly, so simply removing the lid for a short period of time can remove sulphur.
- CO_2 has a stripping effect, so sulphur notes can be removed with further fermentation.
- Certain yeast strains produce more sulphur than others, so your yeast selection is important here.

YEAST AUTOLYSIS

Smells like: Marmite, umami, savoury, meaty.

Causes: Yeast cell death.

The science: Yeast cells burst open upon death, leaking their contents into your beer. Yeast autolysis can occur for a number of different reasons: yeast stress (i.e. yeast cells cooling too quickly or being warmed too quickly); poor yeast storage conditions; and high temperatures (above 25°C/77°F). High alcohol levels and high acidity can also cause yeast cell death.

Commonly found in: Beer packaged with excessive amounts of yeast; any beer where yeast stress has occurred.

How to fix: Yeast autolysis is all about prevention. Take care of your yeast and avoid making any of the errors above!

DIRECTORY

Where to buy homebrew kits, ingredients and equipment.

BARTH HAAS
Hop Pocket Lane
Paddock Wood,
Kent,
TN12 6DQ
www.barthhaasx.com

BEERS OF EUROPE
Garage Lane
Setchey
King's Lynn
Norfolk
PE33 0BE
www.beersofeurope.co.uk

BEERS UNLIMITED
496 London Road
Westcliff-on-Sea
SS0 9LD
01702 345474
www.beersunlimited.co.uk

BREW MART
28 Abbey Lane
Sheffield
S8 0BL
www.brewmart.co.uk

BREW UK
Units 8–9
Sarum Business Park
Lancaster Rd
Old Sarum
Salisbury
SP4 6FB
01722 410705
www.brewuk.co.uk

BREWBITZ
BeerCraft
3 Argyle Street
Pulteney Bridge
Bath
BA2 4BA
01225 448080
www.brewbitz.com

BREWERS DROOP
36 Gloucester Road
Bristol
BS7 8AR
0117 942 7923
www.thebrewersdroop.co.uk

BREWMART
28 Abbey Lane
Sheffield
S8 0BL
0114 2746850
www.brewmart.co.uk

BREWSTORE
61 South Clerk Street
Edinburgh
EH8 9PP
0131 629 0860
www.brewstore.co.uk

BREW2BOTTLE
Units 1&2
Burnley Bridge Business
Park
Magnesium Way
Hapton
BB12 7BF
01254 315082
www.brew2bottle.co.uk

CAMBRIDGE HOMEBREW
127 Milton Road
Cambridge
CB4 1XE
01223 660685
www.camhomeandgarden.
co.uk/homebrew/

CHARLES FARAM
The Hop Store
Monksfield Lane
Newland
Worcestershire
WR13 5BB
www.charlesfaram.co.uk

CROSSMYLOOF
www.crossmyloofbrew.co.uk

GET 'ER BREWED
86 Clonkeen Road
Randalstown
BT41 3JJ
www.geterbrewed.com

HOME BREW HOP SHOP
The Hop Shop
22 Dale Road
Mutley
Plymouth
Devon
PL4 6PE
01752 660382
www.home-brew-hopshop.
co.uk

HOME BREW ONLINE
Unit 9 Harrier Court
Airfield Industrial Estate
Elvington
York
YO41 4EA
01904 791 600
www.home-brew-online.com

LONDON BEER LAB
Arch 41
Nursery Road
SW9 8BP
0208 396 6517
www.londonbeerlab.com

LOVE BREWING
591 Derby Road
Liverpool
L13 8AE
0151 228 8377

Also:
292–294 Chatsworth Road
Chesterfield
Derbyshire
S40 2BY
01246 279382
www.lovebrewing.co.uk

**NORTH DEVON
HOMEBREWS**
50B Bear Street
Barnstaple
Devon
EX32 7DB
01271 374123
www.brewingathome.co.uk

PINTER
Unit 11A
Uplands Business Park
Blackhorse Lane
London
E17 5QJ
www.pinter.co.uk

STOCKS FARM
Suckley
Worcestershire
WR6 5EH
www.stocksfarm.net

THE HOME BREW SHOP
Unit 3
Hawley Lane Business Park
108 Hawley Lane
Farnborough
Hampshire
GU14 8JE
01252 338045
www.the-home-brew-shop.
co.uk

THE MALT MILLER
Unit A2
Faraday Road
Dorcan
Swindon
SN3 5HQ
01793 486 565
www.themaltmiller.co.uk

WATERINTOBEER
Unit 2 Mantle Court
209–211 Mantle Road
Brockley
London
SE4 2EW
www.waterintobeer.co.uk

WHERE TO DRINK

UK

WILD CARD BREWERY BARREL STORE
Unit 7 , Ravenswood Industrial Estate
Shernhall Street
Walthamstow
E17 9HQ

WILD CARD BREWERY & TAPROOM
2 Lockwood Way
Walthamstow
E17 5RB

40FT BREWERY & TAPROOM
2–3 Abbott Street
Dalston
E8 3DP

ORBIT BREWERY
233 Fielding Street
Walworth
SE17 3HJ

TINY REBEL BREWERY BAR
Wern Industrial Estate
Newport
NP10 9FQ

TINY REBEL NEWPORT
22–23 High Street
Newport
NP20 1FX

TINY REBEL CARDIFF
25 Westgate Street
Cardiff
CF10 1DD

NORTH BREWING CO. BREWERY
Springwell
Buslingthorpe Lane
Leeds
LS7 2DF

NORTH BREWING CO. TAP ROOM
3 Sovereign Square
Leeds
LS1 4BA

WILD BEER AT WAPPING WHARF
Units 6–8, Gaol Ferry Steps
Bristol
BS1 6WE

PASTORE BREWING AND BLENDING
Unit 2, Convent Drive
Cambridge
CB25 9QT

UNBARRED BREWERY & TAPROOM
19–23 Elder Place
Brighton
BN1 4GF

TRACK BREWING CO. BREWERY & TAPROOM
Unit 18 , Piccadilly Trading Estate
Manchester
M1 2NP

CASTLE ROCK BREWERY: VAT & FIDDLE PUB
12–14 Queens Bridge Road
Nottingham
NG2 1NB

BELGIUM

MOEDER LAMBIC ORIGINAL
Rue de Savoie 68
1060 Saint-Gilles
www.moederlambic.com

BRASSERIE DE LA SENNE
Drève Anna Boch 19-21
1000 Brussels
www.brasseriedelasenne.be

BIER CIRCUS
57 Rue de L'Enseignement
Brussels
www.bier-circus.be

POECHENELLEKELDER
5 Rue du Chêne
Brussels
www.poechenellekelder.be

NETHERLANDS

PROEFLOKAAL ARENDSNEST
Herengracht 90
1015 BS Amsterdam
www.arendsnest.nl

DRIE DORSTIGE HERTEN
Lange Nieustraat 47
Utrecht
www.dedriedorstigeherten.nl

WILDEMAN
Kolksteeg 3
Amsterdam
www.indewildeman.nl

GERMANY

LEMKE AM SCHLOSS
Luisenplatz 1,
10585 Berlin
www.schloss.lemke.berlin/en/

DAS LEMKE
Dircksenstrasse S–Bahnbogen, 143
10178 Berlin
www.hm.lemke.berlin/en/

BRAUEREI LEMKE BERLIN
Rochstraße 6a,
10178 Berlin
www.lemke.berlin

DENMARK

MIKKELLER BAR
Viktoriagade 8 B–C
1655 København
www.mikkeller.com/locations/mikkeller-viktoriagade

MIKKELLER BAGHAVEN
Refshalevej 169B
1432 København
www.mikkeller.com/locations/mikkeller-baghaven

CZECH REPUBLIC

LYA BEER CAFÉ
Krymská 39
10100 Praha 10–Vršovice
www.lyabeercafe.cz

INDEX

Kyle Books would like to acknowledge and thank the following for supplying photographs for use in this book. Please do contact us should any other additions to the credits be made.

Key: a above, b below, c centre, l left, r right

Alamy Stock Photo 23 all, 29r Nigel Cattlin; 30a & c Philip Dickson; 31a Dorling Kindersley; 43 Nick Moore; 47a Peter Righteous; 63 pixel-shot; 67l ZUMA Press; 78, 82a Phovoir; 81b Wahavi; 81c Biosphoto; 84-5 blickwinkel; 104 picture alliance/ Robert Schlesinger; 144 Cultura RM; 158-9 Arterra Picture Library; 173 Cavan Images

Courtesy of Yakima Valley Hops 51a

Charles Faram & Co Ltd 44 (hop variety shown: Golding UK)

Dreamstime.com 28a James Smart; 28b Maciej Bledowski; 29l Pix569; 31b Peter Hermes Furian; 31c Juan J Alvarez; 33 Lukschen; 36 Wirestock; 46 THPStock; 49a Dmytro Skrypnykov; 49b Michael de Nysschen; 50 Evgeny Vershinin; 61 Mulderphoto; 62 Andris Tcakenko; 67c, 109 Venemama; 71 Andrii Biletskyi; 72 Michele Cornelius; 73 Roger Siljander; 77 Chrupka; 83, 153 Larisabozhikova; 91 Jane Vershinin; 96 Oleg Doroshenko

HPA hops.com.au 46b (hop variety shown: Galaxy®)

iStock 40-41 CaronB; 45a FotoLesnik; 48a typo-graphics; 48b Dora Zett; 57 georgeclerk; 81a lpweber

Science Photo Library 67r Dennis Kunkel Microscopy; 69a Scimat

Shutterstock 21 id-art; 25 paulzhuk; 30b Tsekhmister; 47b Uwe Aranas; 52 Maurizio Milanesio; 87 rawpixel.com; 151 Hans Geel; 163 Vitaliy Kyrychuk; 175 Digieva

Unsplash 79 Brian Taylor

Via **Wikimedia Commons** 107 Smabs Sputzer (1956-2017), CC by 2.0 (https://creativecommons.org/licenses/by/2.0)

Yakima Chief Hops yakimachief.com 45, 51b